CW00495969

Mind Over Chatter: Achieve Mental Clarity and Emotional Health

---

21 Ways to Overcome Overthinking and Enhance Mindfulness Practices in Everyday Life

Sidney Neel

© Copyright 2023 - All rights reserved.

The content contained within this book may not be reproduced, duplicated or transmitted without direct written permission from the author or the publisher.

Under no circumstances will any blame or legal responsibility be held against the publisher, or author, for any damages, reparation, or monetary loss due to the information contained within this book, either directly or indirectly.

Legal Notice:

This book is copyright protected. It is only for personal use. You cannot amend, distribute, sell, use, quote or paraphrase any part, or the content within this book, without the consent of the author or publisher.

Disclaimer Notice:

Please note the information contained within this document is for educational and entertainment purposes only. All effort has been executed to present accurate, up to date, reliable, complete information. No warranties of any kind are declared or implied. Readers acknowledge that the author is not engaged in the rendering of legal, financial, medical or professional advice. The content within this book has been derived from various sources. Please consult a licensed professional before attempting any techniques outlined in this book.

By reading this document, the reader agrees that under no circumstances is the author responsible for any losses, direct or indirect, that are incurred as a result of the use of the information contained within this document, including, but not limited to, errors, omissions, or inaccuracies.

Table of Contents

Introduction

What are you thinking about right now? Of course, you're probably thinking to yourself, "Well, this book..." But, what about the thoughts that are hidden behind your main focus?

What is the background noise of your mind saying? If you were to stop reading and turn to look out the nearest window, what words, ideas, or anxieties would flood your brain? Work stressors? A fight you had with your friend or partner? A low balance in your bank account? An impending deadline? *The existential dread of trying to understand your life's purpose or meaning?*

There's likely something always ticking in the back of your brain, constantly reminding you that there is plenty to worry about. This is what I call mental chatter. While you might be focused on a particular thing at the time, there is a layer of thoughts just waiting to creep up and instill fear, make you second-guess yourself, or even ruin your day.

Our brains are powerful. In fact, they can store the same amount of information as 300 years of TV shows (Harlow, n.d.). Your cerebrum is jam-packed with memories, songs, commercial slogans, hurtful words from bullies, news article titles, faces, sounds, and an endless number of thoughts.

Many of these thoughts are basic and similar to others. How many times a day do you ask yourself, "Did I turn the oven off?" "What should I eat for dinner?" "Did I say something embarrassing at the party last night?" While many of these thoughts are automatic, like the reminder to brush your teeth or wash your hands after going to the bathroom, some of them take up more of our energy than others.

If you're like me, you have been struggling with your thoughts. You might even know that deep down, these thoughts are not productive, true, or anything you should be spending your time thinking about, yet they keep popping up. These thoughts creep into your mind late at night, and they are there waiting for you first thing in the morning. You are bombarded with constant "what ifs," and have stressful arguments and conversations in your mind with yourself and others.

Lucky for you, I've managed to figure out some of the most useful, realistic, and practical methods of calming the chatter. In this book, I have provided 21 methods to reduce overthinking. By developing and nurturing your mental abilities, you will be able to turn the volume down on the anxious thoughts that have been talking over the more rational part of your brain.

As a social interaction specialist and conversation coach, I have seen firsthand how the mental chatter of our minds is often the biggest obstacle we have to overcome to achieve success. Whether you want to start dating new people, making new friends, improving your career, or just get out of the mental prison in your head, overthinking is likely your biggest enemy. We shouldn't be our own bullies. We should be able to create a nurturing and helpful voice that reminds us why we are so special and unique to this world.

By following these 21 techniques, you will be able to gain clarity over why you have these thoughts and where they might've developed. The impression I hope to give to you as you transform into this new stage in life is that it's possible to stay one step ahead of these overpowering emotions.

Overthinking isn't all bad! Sometimes it can help us improve work, prepare for the worst, or learn a greater truth about ourselves. However, overthinking should simply be a tool in our cognitive toolbox—not the driving force in our lives. You will always have certain doubts or hesitations in life, but what's important is putting your best foot forward and knowing how to navigate through which thoughts are empowering and which are debilitating.

The endless stream of anxious thoughts you might be struggling with has likely started to impact your home or work life, which can have devastating effects. If you don't believe you are good enough for a career, or you constantly overthink relationships, you might find that you push others away and create excessive conflict.

I know this because I've been there myself. I've ruined friendships and even partnerships because I was so insecure, I couldn't help but pick fights. There is no telling how many opportunities I missed in the past because I doubted my abilities or assumed that my efforts were futile. Overthinking doesn't just prevent us from getting what we want either. Sometimes it can cause us to take action, but in a way that is just as damaging. For example, impulsive shopping or overeating are common ways to alleviate some of the unwanted emotions associated with overthinking. Not only do these hurt your wallet, but they can also impact your health.

While I know what it feels like to overthink, I also know exactly how to reduce this habit to take back power over your life.

If you are ready to stop the flow of endless thoughts and turn off the faucet that is your mind once and for all, I assure you that I can help. Even if only one of these methods resonates with you, that can still be enough to twist the knob and stop your stream of anxious thoughts. Sure, there might be some leaks in the sink every once in a while, but in this book, I want to provide you with the tools you need to fix whatever pipes burst in the future.

When we are stuck in our minds, it can feel like there is no way out, especially when our thoughts tell us that everything negative we are feeling is true. However, it is possible to slow down your mind to find peace and clarity once and for all.

Now, I'll ask you again: What are you thinking about?

Are you hopeful that you can find change? Are you hesitant that change is possible? There's a good chance that the chatter has already lowered in volume, even if just by one notch. Follow me on this journey to help quiet your mind and find internal peace once and for all.

Chapter 1:

From Overthinking to Mindful Living

Almost one percent of all emergency room visits are related to anxiety. That might not seem like a lot, but the actual numbers show that 1,247,000 people go to the emergency room every year for something related to anxiety (Dark et al, 2016).

We've all experienced anxiety before, but when you're in the thick of it, it's hard to know if what you're experiencing is normal or if there is something more serious going on. Anxiety can often be followed by a plethora of physical symptoms, like racing heart rates, excessive sweating, or headaches. There are many gastrointestinal symptoms associated with anxiety as well, like (Ankrom, 2023):

- diarrhea
- nausea
- cramping
- indigestion
- over or under-eating

Anxiety feels like it starts in our minds. Whenever we begin overthinking, the thoughts loop on top of each other, making it hard to focus and understand our surroundings. But what many of us might not realize is just how impactful overthinking can be on our bodies.

What this means is that you might end up experiencing some very serious bodily symptoms that you don't realize are related to your anxiety. If you're unaware of just how impactful this is on your body, you might end up believing something is going on that is even worse on your body, creating a new issue to worry about. For example, if you are struggling with overthinking about work, it could lead to a stomachache.

Maybe you decide to skip a meal because you're in pain. Later that night, your pain is even worse from being hungry. You go to bed on an empty stomach and wake up feeling tired. Now, not only are you stressed about work, but you might begin to panic that something even more serious is going on. You then ruminate about all the potentials, believing you have a serious health condition all because of a singular anxiety symptom.

Overthinking doesn't just exist in our minds; it grows throughout our body. By recognizing the spiral of thoughts and how it spreads, we can begin to reel in the expansiveness of stress, worry, and panic, making it much easier to manage. The best way to do this is to increase mindfulness.

While many people have heard of mindfulness at some point in their lives, not everyone has a comprehensive overview of what it actually is. In each chapter, I've provided three ways to overcome overthinking and enhance mindfulness practices in everyday life, totaling 21 throughout the seven chapters. By building these methods on top of each other, you can create a solid foundation for quieting the chatter that has been controlling your life.

Utilizing Mindfulness

When we're struggling with mental chatter, it can feel like our thoughts are randomized. It feels like, all of a sudden, you're doing the dishes and anxiety about something that happened when you were in fifth grade pops into your head. You can't help but think about all of the other ways that this connects to your life and how it might make you struggle with insecurity and other challenging aspects of life.

The thing about our thoughts is that they are not as random as they seem. There is a chain reaction that happens, leading to some of the thoughts that you are having. Thoughts aren't singular either. They start attaching to themselves and can grow rapidly like branches off of a tree. Most of our thoughts first happen because of an experience or trigger. This ranges from something big, like receiving news, to something small, such as hearing a random noise in your house. After the experience or initial trigger, there is an emotional response. That emotional response then leads to a mental reaction. Our thoughts are the best way that we can take those mental reactions and feelings and put them into words.

There are so many feelings and emotions that we experience that we can't necessarily describe to other people, let alone ourselves. Because of this, our thoughts can often spiral, causing us to try and figure out how we can remedy that feeling and overcome some of those unwanted emotions. Have you ever noticed that the more stressful a situation or intense a feeling, the more your thoughts start to spiral? We have this internal feeling causing distress and our bodies want that to stop, so we try to use logic and basic understanding to find a resolution.

For example, let's think of a complex emotion like jealousy. Jealousy can happen in obvious circumstances. If you are struggling with money, then you might be jealous of somebody that you see driving a fancy car or wearing designer clothes. You're jealous they have money, and you're jealous that they are in a situation where they can afford things like this. Jealousy is a little bit easier to figure out in this type of scenario; however, it can become more complex when we start to feel these emotions for people we are close with or who are even in similar circumstances as us. For example, imagine a best friend comes to you and says that they are getting engaged or that they're expecting to have a baby soon. You might feel a pang of jealousy. You want, deep down, to be happy for them. You want to celebrate and enjoy this new experience with that other person, but for some reason, you can't help but feel underlying feelings of jealousy.

From that singular instance of them sharing their news, you might start to spiral, and for the next few days or even weeks, you are riddled with insecurity, jealousy, resentment, and other unwanted emotions that are distracting from your day-to-day life. The experience was first the initial moment when their friend shared the news. The emotional response you had was a gut-wrenching feeling. You felt insecure, uncertain, and even a little upset. Your mental reaction is then to start trying to contextualize these deep mental feelings and putting them into thoughts and words. You might start comparing yourself to other people and their life circumstances. You might start to go back through your life's history and consider all of the different decisions and actions you could have taken to have a completely different life.

This is just one example of how a singular experience can spiral and branch off in a multitude of ways. Sometimes, these experiences happen frequently, and sometimes it only takes one singular instance to start our spiraling thoughts. If you get a work email or text that says your boss wants to meet with you, all of a sudden you might start spiraling about your job. You wonder if you're going to end up losing your job. *Did you mess up at work the other day? Are they calling to yell at you or reprimand you?* In reality, they're simply letting you know that maybe a coworker called off, or perhaps they're asking if you can take on an extra task for your next shift. It might be something extremely minor, but our thoughts can keep reproducing and building on top of each other because that initial feeling isn't something that we are necessarily focusing on. Our mental reaction can, therefore, shape our next experience, which will then lead to even more rumination over the past or future and anxiety in the present.

Before you know it, you are rolling down a hill with no way to stop yourself from spiraling into deeper and darker territories. How can we stop this spiral? How can we stop one single thought from turning into a forest of trees with branches stemming into different territories of our mind?

The best way to do this is by utilizing mindfulness. Mindfulness is the practice of raising awareness of the present situation. It is how you can pay attention to your surroundings and do so in a neutral way. You might think to yourself, "I'm mindful all the time. I'm always freaking out about my heart racing or the way that I look. I'm always paying attention to how people are talking to me or reacting to me." This is one aspect of awareness. This is spatial awareness, however, not necessarily mindfulness.

Beyond that, it's also important to have social and emotional awareness. Social awareness is the recognition that other people are also experiencing their situation. Sometimes it feels as though we're aware, but really, we're centering ourselves in the situation. We are not always the center of everybody's focus, even when it feels like it. Anxiety, especially social anxiety, can make us focus on ourselves and how we might be influencing the situation, when in reality, others are not paying attention to what we're doing and are more focused on themselves.

It's also important to have emotional awareness, and a huge aspect of this form of awareness is withholding judgment. For example, if you're in the middle of a party, and you're thinking to yourself, "Oh my hair looks messed up, I'm sweaty and shaky. All my friends are looking at me weird and they're judging me," it might feel like you're aware at this moment. You're hyper-aware of yourself and the way that you look, but you're not being mindful at this moment.

Mindfulness would start with that initial awareness, and you might think to yourself, "I'm feeling sweaty and shaky," but then after that, mindfulness requires withholding judgment. It's noticing that you're in this present moment. This would include thoughts like, "Other people are around me. They might be looking at me. They might be interacting with me, and I might be influencing the situation, but I am simply here in this present moment."

Mindfulness is a way that we can reel in our thoughts and focus on being as neutral, empathetic, compassionate, and present as possible. Presence is the biggest distinction between mindfulness and simply feeling as though you are aware of the moment. Being mindful means being present in the hours, minutes, and seconds that are passing; not existing in the past or future. Mindfulness can stop the thought loop because you can become aware that you are spiraling rather than giving into your negative thoughts.

Mindfulness is a practice that takes time to master; however, there are many small ways that you can begin to implement mindfulness into your life. The first is to simply pay attention to your spatial awareness, look at your physical surroundings, and identify different things that are in the room with you at this present moment.

One activity to do is to identify everything in the room that has a specific color. Let's try this right now. Identify everything in the room that is the color red. You might see a book or, perhaps, a mug sitting on the coffee table. Maybe you see a potted plant that is in a red container. Maybe you have a red throw pillow on your couch. Let's keep traveling through the rainbow. What in the room is orange, yellow, green, blue, and purple? Now consider other colors like pink, white, gray, or brown. Don't stress yourself out about trying to find every little thing that is a certain color. Mindfulness is not a game where you have to reach a certain threshold or get a certain score. Mindfulness is all about simply noticing your surroundings and sitting through the moment!

Notice any judgments, assumptions, or conclusions that you try to make as you're looking at things around you. For example, you might look at the mug on the coffee table and think to yourself, "That mug is dirty. It's been sitting there for a few days. I need to clean it up. I'm so messy. I wish the house wasn't so cluttered."

As you can see, a simple trigger, like a dirty mug, can lead to a spiral of negative thoughts. Mindfulness is simply noticing the mug, and moving on. Stop the spiral of thoughts by moving on to the next thing rather than judging yourself. You might look at the throw pillow sitting on the couch and think, "That's such an ugly throw pillow. I have such bad taste. I need to buy new things for my home." You might notice the book sitting on the shelf and think to yourself, "I need to start reading more. I'm really bad at reading. I'm so dumb. I wish I was smarter."

All of these things are forms of judgment that can break down our self-esteem and make us feel defeated. Mindfulness involves simply noticing these little things and moving past them. Another great form of mindfulness to utilize is to hold an ice cube in your hand and watch it melt. The next time that you are feeling panicked or as though your thoughts are suffocating you, walk to your freezer, grab an ice cube, hold it in your hands, and feel all of the sensations. Watch as it changes shapes. Roll it across your fingers and switch from one hand to the other. By the time the ice melts, you will notice that the thought loop has stopped. Like the ice cube, your thoughts will melt away until there is nothing left.

Sometimes, after we're done with these little mindfulness activities, our thoughts go right back to where they were before. You might start another spiral again, but that means it's time to utilize another mindfulness activity. If you are worried about work, you might be stressed about all of the things that could go wrong tomorrow. Rather than letting the spiral continue, identify everything in the room that is red. After this, you'll notice that the spiral stops. You can start moving on to the next thing that requires your focus.

If your thought goes back to work, move down the rainbow and keep identifying colors. Take it up a notch and start identifying textures. What *are some items* in the room that are made out of fabric? What is metal, and what might be wood? What might be a painted surface? You can also simply look at the thing right in front of you and identify this. For example, if the thing right in front of you is your phone or tablet, what's a characteristic of this item? Is it black and shiny? Are there any other things in the room that are black and shiny? It feels uncomfortable at first, and in a way, mindfulness almost seems too easy. However, as you keep practicing, it will eventually click. You will realize that by pulling your focus from your thoughts and mental chatter to the space around you, it becomes easier to then reduce the mental chatter.

The Practice of Breathing

How are you holding your body right now? Part of building spatial awareness is recognizing the space that we are currently in, and that space includes you. How are you holding your body within this space? Remember to withhold judgment. When we think about spatial awareness and how we exist in the space, our first thought might go to your size or appearance. You might start judging yourself. Maybe you're slouching with your legs spread open, and perhaps you're thinking that you're sitting terribly or that you have poor posture. Withhold your judgment and notice your body, how it's placed, and how that is contributing to the way that you feel. Right now, take your shoulders and roll them backward.

Pretend as though your shoulders are like a clock and roll them backward toward your spine in a counterclockwise pattern. Then, straighten your spine and puff your chest out. Doing this alone can change the way that you feel within a space. Now, place your feet flat on the ground. Spread your knees shoulder-width apart and relax your hips. Once you do this, take a big deep breath in. After you reposition yourself, you might automatically feel your body wanting to take a big deep breath. Start by pulling your breath in through your nose and feel it deep in your gut, all the way down to your belly button.

Place your hand on your stomach, just above your belly button, and hold your breath for a moment. Now, slowly and steadily, let it out through a small hole in your mouth. As you do this, relax your shoulders, abdomen, and spine. Make sure your knees and hips are still as relaxed as possible. Deep breathing is an excellent way to help us stop the flow of our thoughts. This is a mindfulness technique that we can use to raise awareness of our body in the moment. Sometimes, the way that we are holding our body can contribute to even more anxiety and stress. You might notice that when you are in a social interaction or trying to complete a stressful work project, you're clenching your jaw or making a fist. Our body has natural reactions to our thoughts and sometimes these can contribute to even more stress.

This reaction is known as a stress response. Most living things have a stress response, as it's a necessary survival tactic that ensures that we survive any sort of threat to our health or body. Picture humans thousands of years ago, before we had the comfort of our homes, security cameras, and other types of weapons to keep us safe. We were left on our own to defend ourselves. We also didn't have grocery stores with food sources, so this meant we had to go out in the wild to hunt and forage for our food, much like many private primates still do in the wild to this day.

There are many things wired within us to keep us safe as we seek the things we need. We don't just walk forward without hesitation into the thick of the woods; we take careful steps to ensure that we don't fall off high ledges or step into a swampy or wet area. If you hear tree branches break in the distance, you might look around to make sure that you're not being stalked by a bear or other predator. If you notice the clouds start to turn gray and you hear thunder, you might seek shelter to protect yourself from the rain. All of these small things are naturally wired within us to help keep us safe. Even as babies, we were born with strong grips to help us hold on to our mother and ensure that we can stay as protected as possible. All humans have vulnerabilities and it's within our biology to make sure that we try to keep ourselves safe.

In modern times, we don't necessarily need the same survival skills. You don't have to go hunt and forage for food. You can order it to your house with the tap of a few buttons on your phone. You might even have somebody who provides food for you, and you don't even have to worry about grocery shopping or meal planning.

We have homes with security cameras and strong locks, and some of us even have weapons to ensure that if somebody were to come and try to break into our home, we would be protected. We have entire systems meant to keep us safe such as laws, regulations, and law enforcement. Of course, sometimes these things fail and we end up getting hurt anyway. However, it's safe to say that we can be a lot more at peace now than we used to be.

The thing is our genetics have not quite caught up with that. We can still feel intense stress and panic, just as we did thousands of years ago. The threats to our survival look a lot different now than they used to. Rather than worrying about getting attacked by a bear in the woods, we have to worry about getting fired by our bosses so that we can pay our bills and keep food on the table. Rather than trying to prove our strength to fit in with a tribe or small community, we post on social media about it to make sure that we are admired and fit in with our online peers.

Life today looks a lot different than it did years ago, but our biology is very similar. The stress response still exists. When you feel overwhelmed with panic or worry, your stress response might get triggered, leading you to want to react in similar ways. The stress response keeps us protected by preparing us for whatever threat we might have to battle.

There are two common forms of the stress response known as the flight or fight response. The flight response is one in which we would run away from the danger to try and seek safety. The fight response is one where we would fight that threat. Many animals have this fight or flight response and you will see it in various ways. For example, if a bird is in front of you, if you take a step toward it, it might fly away as a flight response. If you see a snake and you step toward it, it might lunge at you and try to bite you as a fight response. Humans have both, and from person to person, what kind of response we lead with differs.

There are other types of stress responses as well, such as the freeze response. This is something we do to help us try and stay still in the moment so as not to entice more threats. It's also simply a natural reaction we have when we can't go anywhere else or take other actions. You'll see this response in children who are in abusive situations. They can't fight their parents and they can't run away either, so often, the only thing that they're able to do is freeze in that moment and try their best to survive. Another response you'll often see is the fawn response, where the person threatened tries to appease the threat to prevent any more trauma. You will see this in abusive relationships. The victim might do their best to try and make their abuser happy to prevent more abuse from being inflicted.

Regardless of the type of stress response we have, similar things happen within our body when we are triggered to respond with either a fight or flight reaction. First and foremost, your body might tense up. You might make a fist. You might feel tension in your arms, shoulders, abdomen, or legs. In addition, your heart rate will likely kick in and start beating faster. You will also notice your breathing becomes more rapid or shallow. This is all to ensure that we are prepared to fight or flee right away, no matter what threat occurs.

Interestingly, most of the modern threats we have to deal with don't require fight or flight. Getting a stressful email from your boss is not remedied by you punching away that email. You can't run away from that email either—your phone is still something that you have to use. You can ignore the email, but ultimately that email is still going to be in your inbox and the work problem will persist.

When we feel stress and that stress has nowhere to go, it sits inside of our body and builds and builds, leading to more anxiety and background mental chatter. To help you achieve mental clarity, one thing you can do is to soothe that stress response through breathing. Deep breathing is important to remind your body that you are okay. As you start to reduce that initial stress response, you can then think more clearly so that you can take action against whatever stressor has been presented to you. The stress response impacts your breathing, so if you lead with deep breathing first, you will then find yourself calming down and realizing that the threat isn't as bad as it seems.

Deep breathing is something that we should do as soon as we start feeling anxious. One way to do this is to simply breathe in through your nose and out through your mouth. As you're breathing, try and count to help keep your mind focused as well. Breathe into your nose as you count to three and breathe out through your nose as you count down from three. You might also count from one to five if you notice that your breathing is faster.

Find a pace that works for you. It helps to place your hand on your stomach and feel yourself breathing to remind your entire body that everything is going to be okay. It's also very helpful to practice deep breathing exercises throughout the day, even when you're not feeling anxious to help regulate your bodily systems. This means waking up in the morning and taking some deep breaths for 15 to 30 minutes to help relax your mind as you wake up. You could also practice deep breathing before you go to bed at night to calm your mind down so you can get a good night's sleep. Breathing is something we do all day long without thinking about it, but as you start to increase mindfulness, raise awareness over your breathing patterns.

You will notice that by focusing on the way that you're breathing, it becomes much easier to reduce mental chatter. Sometimes you might realize that you've gone an hour with shallow breaths, or that you're holding your breath through moments when you are experiencing extreme stress. Take a step away from whatever is causing you to panic and feel your lungs inhale and exhale.

Meditation for Beginners

Mindfulness and breathing can seem a lot simpler on paper, but they're a little bit harder to practice in person. Our minds are very good at convincing us that our stressors are very real and something that we need to panic about. The stress response usually takes priority in your brain because, at the end of the day, we care most about survival. Our brains don't always think long-term. For example, when you're hungry, you might reach for the quickest and easiest meal even though it's not the most nutritious. We know at the end of the day that it's important to eat full, nutritious meals, but sometimes, we reach for a quick and sugary or fatty snack to help satisfy our craving right away. Our brains think short-term. They want us to stop being hungry as soon as possible, rather than trying to plan long, more difficult, or complex nutritious meals.

Our brains are very focused on our stressors, therefore making it more difficult to work through that intense anxiety. To help make mindfulness a more active and natural part of your life. One thing you can use is meditation. Meditation is kind of a combination of breath work and mindfulness and is a practice that requires you to step away from your regular life demands and take a moment to sit with your thoughts as you quiet your mind.

There are many preconceived notions of what it means to meditate, such as making your brain feel empty. Meditation also has some mystical associations. You might have seen the image of somebody sitting cross-legged and levitating in the air. That is not the case! Meditation can be done anywhere, at any time. All that's required is your complete focus, and preferably a quiet space away from others.

Meditation is the act of sitting with your thoughts and watching them as they pass by. Consider it like watching a pasture of wild horses, with the horses representing your thoughts. Rather than running up to a horse, jumping on its back, and going for a ride, simply sit back and watch the horses graze in the pasture. Step outside of your body and outside of your thoughts. Close your eyes and picture yourself standing outside your home, looking in through the window rather than sitting inside of your body. These are ways we can start to think of ourselves—not necessarily detached from our thoughts, but not driven by them either. They are a part of us, but they do not define us. They are a product of our experiences, emotions, and life in general, but they are not the conclusive summary of who we are as people.

Meditation isn't the act of silencing your thoughts, stifling them, or suppressing them. It's simply noticing them and withholding judgment or preventing yourself from taking action on these thoughts. Meditation can take a while to master, which is why it's important to practice it regularly. If you're somebody who struggles with intense rumination and mental chatter, try practicing meditation daily. You don't have to spend hours meditating! Start with five minutes a day for a week. By week two, try and do 10 minutes a day; and by week three, do 30 minutes a day. By the end of the month, you will discover that it's easy for you to practice meditating for about 30 minutes a day.

As you start to reduce mental chatter, you can also reduce your meditation sessions. You might find yourself simply doing it for an hour or two a week, and that's fine! There's no requirement as to how long you need to meditate or how much you should practice it. What's important is making it a consistent part of your routine at first so that it becomes more natural for you to learn how to disconnect and sit with your thoughts as they pass by.

To meditate, ensure that you find a place without distraction. Some of us live in really small homes or even studio apartments, so we can't dedicate an entire area to meditating. However, simply find a place that you don't sit in that often. For example, sit at the end of your bed instead of sitting closer to the front. You might even sit on the ground next to the couch rather than sitting on the couch. If you find a new space that you don't normally sit in, it will make it easier for your brain to snap into a meditative state. We often associate certain locations with certain activities, making it harder for our brains to disconnect from our thoughts for the time being. For example, if you sit at the kitchen table, you might find yourself feeling hungry and wanting to grab a snack. If you sit on the recliner where you normally watch TV, you might find yourself reaching for the remote and putting on your favorite show. If you find yourself sitting in your bed, you might have the urge to lie down and fall asleep.

Meditate in a space that's different from where you normally sit to help your brain create a new mindset. As you're meditating, focus on your body and make sure your legs, hips, shoulders, and stomach are all relaxed. Then, start deep breathing. Don't count at first. Simply get into a pattern that works for you. After that, you can then start counting. There are also many free forms of guided meditation online that you can use. This uses a scripted voice to help you travel through your thoughts to prevent you from spiraling.

Your first few meditation sessions might be a little bit more challenging because you've been dealing with a lot of built-up mental chatter! As you continue practicing, eventually, you'll be able to meditate completely on your own. Once you notice a thought popping into your brain, don't travel down that path. Simply let it pass by. Withhold judgment and don't make yourself feel bad because you have negative or intense thoughts. Think of them like leaves floating on top of a river. Simply watch as they pass by and don't reach out and grab one. Don't try to clear the river of all the leaves, just simply notice as they appear in your vision and travel downstream.

You can also think of them like clouds in the sky. Watch as they change shapes and disappear over time. Eventually, you might notice that the stream becomes more clear and the sky becomes less cloudy. Do your best to focus on your breathing and your body as you continue to meditate.

Chapter Review

Turning the volume down on the background noise in our head starts when we look internally. Earmuffs and louder noises might drown out the noise, but to reduce the chatter, it requires us to find the volume button inside of our mind.

To help you raise mental awareness, remember to follow the methods below:

1. **Raise awareness of your spatial surroundings:** What makes up the area you're in? How are you sitting? How does the furniture sit in the room? Who is with you? Start with a basic understanding of awareness within the physical space you are in. Pay attention to what is running through your mind. Do these productive thoughts require action, or are you ruminating on the same thing? If you find yourself ruminating, you can then take the next steps to power through with more mindfulness.

2. **Take a big deep breath in and relax your shoulders:** Remember to notice how your stress response is being activated and take a moment to remind yourself you are okay. You are not dying and nothing bad is happening—you are simply overwhelmed with mental chatter.

3. **Make meditation a regular part of your routine:** Find a place you feel safe and comfortable in and set a timer for just five minutes to help you focus on your breathing and thoughts.

Remember that quieting the chatter doesn't mean having to silence it. Sometimes you might find yourself still listening in. The most important thing is to remember that these thoughts do not have to control you and your actions.

Mindfulness is made of three parts: spatial awareness, emotional awareness, and social awareness, so the first and easiest awareness to raise is spatial awareness. The remainder of the chapters will focus on social and mental awareness to help you look at your mental chatter and break apart what has been happening inside your brain. However, if we lack spatial awareness, it can be hard to get a true and objective understanding of the social and mental aspects.

Raising awareness within the present moment by identifying your surroundings is also a form of mindfulness. It's a reminder that you are right here, in this present moment, and this is the only place you really *need* to be. Once you master this realization, the rest of the mental chatter silencing will come back into place.

Chapter 2:

Finding Mental Clarity Through Self-Reflection

I remember a time when my anxiety was at its worst. I was overwhelmed with work and spent hours at my job, yet I was still struggling with money and to make ends meet. My bills were too high, and my income just wasn't enough to keep up. I was overworked and underpaid, and it sucked every ounce of motivation in me. I was tired, groggy, and easily annoyed.

This started to impact my relationships. I was too tired to hang out with my friends and didn't have the money to do some of the things they wanted to do, even when I had the time to socialize. I was neglecting my romantic relationship, leaving little joy in my life. I felt isolated and alone, and often found myself stuck in my head.

I would overthink about bills, and whether or not I was doing good enough at my job. If I didn't do well, I would lose my job, meaning it would be even harder to keep up financially. I worried about missing payments and debt piling up. I worried that I would ruin my reputation and have to start over. I worried I would lose all my friends or that my partner would leave me. Overthinking was plaguing every part of my life, and it wasn't going away. In fact, it was growing and growing, making everything worse each day.

One day, my mind and body had enough. I was in the bathroom at work when I started to feel dizzy. I had a jolt of pain shoot up my spine and thought I was going to fall over. I felt sick and ended up throwing up in the toilet. I stumbled out of the bathroom and my coworker took one look at me before asking what was wrong. I explained my pain and how I could hear and feel my heartbeat in every part of my skull. The lights were so bright and painful that I could barely open my eyes, and I thought I was going to throw up again. She told me that I was likely having a migraine. I had never had one before and always thought they were just a type of headache, but this was different. She offered to drive me home, and I had no choice but to agree.

The migraine faded, but it came back two or three times a week for the next couple of months. It was making work harder to keep up with, and I didn't know what to do. I finally had enough and went to see a doctor, where I was diagnosed with anxiety and migraine attacks and referred to a therapist.

This was a major realization for me. I was so worried about every aspect of life that I created a new problem with my health. I genuinely thought something more serious was going on and that I had a rare neurological condition. While migraines can be serious, they are manageable through various coping mechanisms.

If you are like me, don't wait until your overthinking gets to this painful point to do something about it. Sometimes, we have to go through these tough experiences to finally face ourselves. It isn't until you are forced to look in the mirror that you really grasp just how much overthinking can take over your life.

Rather than letting overthinking transform into an anxiety disorder, stay one step ahead and foster healthy self-reflection through these mindfulness techniques.

Self-reflection is a way we can take mindfulness and apply it to the world around us.

Identifying Thought Patterns

When someone says a certain word or phrase, does that make you think of a song? When you see a certain object or color, does that make you think of a certain person? We have a lot of associations in our brains that we can connect to the world around us. These can sometimes be referred to as patterns of thought. When you smell a certain dish, you might think of your mom who used to cook this dish all the time. When you see something on the street, like a bird or a specific car, you might recall somebody who's connected to this item.

Sometimes, patterns of thought can turn into things that hold us back or keep us stagnant. These can be referred to as "cognitive distortions." A cognitive distortion is a pattern of thought that perpetuates overthinking. These types of patterns of thought become so habitual and ingrained into our everyday thought process that we might not realize just how detrimental they are to our overall mental health.

One of the most common and easy-to-understand types of cognitive distortions is overgeneralization. This is when we take one thought or idea and spin it into large assumptions and negative types of thinking. For example, let's say you and your friend are going out to eat at a restaurant. As they go to order their favorite meal, the person working tells them that they are out of a specific ingredient. All of a sudden, your friend starts to get really angry and upset. They order something else and after leaving the restaurant, they keep complaining. They keep going on about how nothing works out for them, everything is terrible, and life is a bad place. They start recalling all of the other times that they experienced this type of negative situation and all of a sudden, one missing ingredient in a restaurant dish turns into a night filled with misery. This would be an example of overgeneralization.

Bad things happen all the time, but when you're struggling with overgeneralization, sometimes those bad things—no matter how small—can become inflated and turn into large worldviews. Once you start cherry-picking all of the negativity that you've experienced in life, it's really easy to assume that the world is a very bleak and negative place.

The opposite of this type of cognitive distortion isn't necessarily the best route to take either. It's okay to have bad things happen and acknowledge that they are undesirable experiences. You don't have to stay positive in the face of everything negative that you experience; however, when we conflate these small things over and over again, it can really wear us down and turn into an automatic negative perspective.

For example, if you wake up late one morning for work, and you end up becoming stressed and overwhelmed as you try to head out the door, it's okay to recognize that this is a really stressful and frustrating time. However, if you are struggling with overgeneralization, then for the remainder of the day, you might be upset and focus on negativity. You get to work, and every little thing is bothering you, and you're highlighting all of the terrible attributes associated with your job.

It's not like you have to think to yourself, "Oh, it's so great that I'm running late." However, if you start thinking things like, "My life is the worst... I'm such a bad person for always running late.... I hate my life," then that's going to make it difficult for you to stay objective and realistic in the face of these minor struggles.

Another form of cognitive distortion includes black-and-white thinking, which is also referred to as "all-or-nothing thinking." This is when we categorize everything in an either/or box. For example, if you have the mindset that you need to get first place at a competition or else you're a failure, that can perpetuate black-and-white thinking. You can still get second, third, fourth, or fifth place and be successful and talented. However, those who struggle with all-or-nothing mindsets feel like they're failures when they don't get their desired results.

This type of mindset makes us think that we have to be the prettiest, smartest, and funniest person in our social circle. Black-and-white thinking makes us think that if we are not rich, we are failures; or if we do not have the best job, then we are losers.

All-or-nothing thinking can also impact your habits. For example, if you're trying to start a new diet, you might decide to give up sweets and all sugary drinks and snacks. On day two of your diet, you cave in and drink a sugary soda. You then think to yourself, "What's the point of even dieting? I should just give up... I'm such a failure." You could still come back from this and continue with your health regimen, but instead, someone who perpetuates black-and-white thinking sees these minor setbacks as total failures and reasons to give up.

Another type of cognitive distortion is catastrophizing. This is when we assume the worst and perpetuate anxiety over this worst-case scenario. For example, if you struggle with the fear of flight, you might never get on an airplane because you think it's going to crash. If you're afraid of driving, you might never get behind the wheel of a car because you assume that you're going to have an accident.

Catastrophizing can prevent us from doing things that we want in life, like applying for new jobs or going on dates and meeting new people. When we struggle with catastrophizing, we are fixated on the worst-case scenario, when in reality, most of the time, these bad things don't happen.

The last cognitive distortion to discuss is personalization. This involves us placing ourselves at the center of conflict and other situations, usually leaving us feeling bad about ourselves. For example, if you're at a party and you spill your drink, you might assume the night is ruined and that everybody had a bad time because of one small mistake you made. For the most part, everybody forgets that you even spilled a drink in the first place, yet you can't help but replay that scenario in your mind over and over again.

If you are having a bad hair day and feeling insecure about the way that you look, you might walk into your classroom and a couple of people give you a weird look. You then assume that they must be thinking about you and your hairstyle, and judging you for the way that you look. The thing about cognitive distortions is that we all struggle with them from time to time. Everybody's had the fear that they're going to get in an accident when getting on a plane or in a car. All of us have had moments where we're insecure and hyper-fixated on how other people are looking at us. However, the thing about cognitive distortions is that when we struggle with multiple different kinds on a day-to-day basis, this can clutter up the voice in our head, leading to excessive mental chatter.

If you relate to any of these types of thought patterns, then you need to start identifying them consistently. One of the best ways to help you identify and overcome these different thought patterns is through the use of journaling.

Creating Your Journal

When was the last time you wrote about how you're feeling? For some of us, journaling may be something that we're already doing, but for others, you might not have taken your thoughts to pen and paper since you were in elementary school or earlier. Journaling is a great way to help us get our thoughts down on paper and understand them in a brand-new way.

Journaling does not have to be done in the traditional sense that we think of. When we imagine journaling, we might picture ourselves sitting down with a pen and notebook and starting with "*Dear diary...*" That doesn't have to be the case at all!

No one's going to be reading your journal. You don't have to try and impress anybody. There are endless ways that you can try to get your thoughts out of your head. Also, digital journaling can be beneficial to people who struggle with writing, especially if you are constantly working on a computer. You can have an extra document open and pull it up to write down your thoughts. Have it be a little place where you can make notes and reminders to yourself throughout the day. You don't have to necessarily reflect on everything that you've been through, nor do you have to get deep and share all your secrets. Sometimes, we can just jot down different notes and ideas like:

- I'm feeling anxious after a conversation with a friend.
- I feel frustrated that my partner hasn't texted me back.
- I can't stop thinking about that embarrassing thing I did the other day.

We can give ourselves sort of reminders for the future like:

- Your anxiety is going to pass.
- Everything is going to be okay.
- This will work out better than you can imagine.

There are endless ways to journal, and you can explore all these types of options so that you can find something that works best for you and your needs.

The biggest benefit of journaling is that it can help you make sense of your emotions. Sometimes when we bottle things up and hold onto them, we don't see them for what they are. For example, if you're struggling because you've been annoyed or frustrated with your partner lately, you might feel like there are endless things that you can complain about. You start wondering if you're not meant to be together and maybe you don't love them as much as you thought. However, once you actually get these words out and write them down, you might realize that they were just anxious thoughts. They aren't the truth, and they aren't anything definitive that you need to take action on. They're just natural thoughts that occur because we've been taught throughout our lives to reflect on relationships in this way.

Journaling is also a great way for you to talk to somebody else and say everything that's on your mind without actually saying it to them. For example, if you're frustrated with a friend, you could write them a letter and tell them how angry you are. After you're done, you can tear the letter up or burn it to help you let go of some of those anxieties and resentments that you've been holding on to. You might discover that you actually do want to tell them all these things after you finish writing them down, and now you have a script to make these difficult conversations easier. Journaling will help you get your emotions out rather than holding onto them.

Another great use for journaling is to store your anxiety for later. For example, let's say you're at work one day and your boss comes up to you and says, "We need to have a meeting and I want to have a conversation with you. Can you meet me later today at five?" You agree to the meeting, but they don't give any details as to what the conversation is about. You can't help but think about all the negative outcomes and you might start struggling with overgeneralization or jumping to conclusions. You can write down what you're feeling and walk away from this to help you take a break from overthinking. Write down: *I feel anxious because I don't know what the meeting is about.*

You can also start listing some of your symptoms, like: *I feel very distracted and it's hard for me to focus on my work because I'm so anxious. I'm scared that the meeting is going to go badly.* Then, you can close your notebook, put it in a drawer, and let go of that anxiety temporarily.

This is a great way to help you declutter your brain when the chatter is overwhelming and increasingly distracting you from the tasks that require your attention. Later, after the meeting, you realize that it wasn't anything that serious. Your boss just wanted to tell you that you've been doing great so far, and they really liked your performance. You head back to your office and pull out that notebook, crossing off those anxieties. By the time you go back to these anxious notes, you'll realize that the situation resolved itself anyway.

Another type of journaling that can be beneficial is free writing. This involves setting a timer and then writing down as many thoughts that come to your mind as possible within this specific timeframe. Start with five minutes and work your way up to 10 or 15. Once the timer starts, write everything that comes to mind. You don't have to worry about punctuation or capitalization. You don't have to worry about spelling words correctly or even finishing sentences. Just write down everything that comes to your mind and jot it down as fast as you can. Then, afterward, you can go back through and review what you wrote. You can pick things apart or elaborate and expand on them. This is a great way to sort of dump a lot of the clutter that's been filling up your mind.

To help you start journaling more, set a specific time to journal every day. The best time to do this is before you go to bed at night or when you wake up in the morning. When you journal before you go to bed, it helps you get a lot of your thoughts out, which could contribute to more restful sleep. If you journal first thing in the morning, it can help set the tone for the day and get you started on the right track so that your mind is clear and peaceful as you navigate your different responsibilities throughout the day.

Journaling can be hard for some people, especially when we don't have a lot of practice putting our thoughts and feelings into words. Journal prompts or reflection questions are a great way to get you thinking about what's going on in your mind a little bit more. Below are some reflection questions and journal problems to help overthinkers get started with the journaling practice:

- What is your biggest anxiety?
- What is a thought you ruminate on frequently?
- What is a past anxious memory that you struggle to let go of?
- What is the biggest coping mechanism you have?
- What is something that always makes you feel better?
- What is your biggest insecurity?
- Who is someone you admire?
- Who is someone you have struggled with the most in life?
- Who is someone you feel safe talking about your struggles with?
- Where do you feel safest?
- What do you remember most about your childhood?
- What is one thing you've learned about yourself as an adult?
- If you could redo one memory, what would it be?
- Why has it been difficult to overcome mental chatter?

- If you had one wish, what would it be?
- What is your biggest fear?
- What do you hope for yourself in the next decade?
- If you could glimpse into the future, 10 years from now, what is one thing that would disappoint you to see? What is the biggest thing you would hope to see?

There are many journal prompts and reflection questions you can find online, and exploring your thoughts can be done in a multitude of ways. When journaling, try to remember to keep track of the date and time. This way, you can revisit the prompt later on to see how your thoughts might've changed or notice patterns in thinking around specific times.

Affirmations From Negative to Positive

When was the last time you said to yourself, "I got this"? When was the last time you were able to look in the mirror and say, "Everything is going to be okay today"?

For some of us, this might have never happened before in our lives. For other people, you might have regular mantras that you tell yourself to help break through the mental chatter. Either way, these are known as affirmations.

Affirmations are declarations that we say in our heads. When we repeat these affirmations over time, we eventually come to believe them and recognize that they are truthful. They often are opinionated, and they vary from person to person. Most of the time, people lead with negative affirmations. We don't even realize that we're saying them to ourselves, and they often arise based on many different triggers.

Negative affirmations include statements like:

- Everything is terrible.
- My life sucks.
- I am not good at my job.
- I'm not good at anything.
- I have nothing to offer.
- I have no value.

As you can see, these can be very damaging statements. Reading them from another perspective might help you realize just how harmful they can be. However, you might have found yourself repeating these on an almost daily basis. Can you think of some negative affirmations that you consistently tell yourself now?

Negative affirmations usually rely on the use of extremes. This means saying things like always/never, everything/nothing, or best/worst. For example, you might think to yourself:

- I'm always failing.
- I never had anything good happen in my life.
- I am the worst person I know.
- Everything is bad.
- Nothing seems to go right.

These statements use absolute phrases that create sweeping and drastic summaries. As you continue to repeat these, they branch off into even more types of negative affirmations. Then, before you know it, the entirety of the voice in your head is upholding these damaging beliefs.

Repeating negative affirmations to yourself day after day makes you more likely to become influenced by your negative thoughts and, therefore, take action because of them. It can be awkward and uncomfortable to try and switch negative affirmations to positive ones, but doing so can help you rewrite the script that's been directing your life.

You've likely heard of positive affirmations before. These involve sayings like:

- I am valued.
- I am loved.
- I am talented.
- I am smart.
- I am intelligent.
- I am brave.

One thing you can do to help make the transition more comfortable is to use neutral affirmations. Neutral affirmations are more on the objective side of things and are based on truth, making it harder for you to fight them. For example, if you tell yourself "I am loved," then you might start a little argument in your head with yourself, thinking about all the people who have wronged you or who have done negative things to you in the past. However, neutral affirmations are a little bit harder to fight or break down the validity of, therefore, they create a stronger basis for us to eventually transition into positive affirmations. Examples of neutral affirmations include:

- I am alive.
- I have people in my life and around me.
- I have a job.
- I have a career.
- I have money in my bank account.

- I have health on my side.
- I have survived so far.
- I am safe.
- I am protected.
- Nothing bad is going to happen to me.
- Everything is going to work out.

After a while, you can eventually turn these into more positive affirmations. For example, "Everything is going to work out" can be a calming and safe neutral affirmation but make it a little bit more positive by saying "Everything is going to work out in my favor." Saying something like "Nothing bad is going to happen to me," can also make you feel safe and protected. Change that into something more positive by saying, "Something good is going to happen to me."

Take some time to write down neutral, negative, and positive affirmations in your journal. Once you start writing down your negative affirmations, you'll realize just how harsh and unfair they can be. Would you say these things to somebody that you love? Chances are likely not, so we must learn how to stop saying them to ourselves.

Neutral affirmations can be a little bit harder to think of at first, but as you continue practicing, you'll be able to find some really powerful ones that make you feel better and help reduce mental chatter. Positive affirmations can, again, feel a little bit uncomfortable at first, but over time, you'll realize that they can be very helpful in making you feel better.

Write these down in your journal! Write them on Post-it notes and put them on your mirror or even turn them into artwork, like by getting a tattoo or painting one and framing it to put on your wall. Anytime you can remind yourself of some of the positivity in life, it gets easier to help push through some of the mental chatter that keeps us stuck in the same place.

Chapter Review

When the same thoughts are repeated day after day, they all start to blur together. They create an internal voice, and deciphering whether that voice is right or wrong can be confusing. Sometimes, it feels like our worst thoughts are true and our best thoughts are lies; but, what matters is that we focus on productive thoughts that help drive us to get the things we want and overcome what is holding us back.

This can be done in three powerful ways:

1. **Identify the common thought patterns you struggle with:** Do you find yourself making assumptions or jumping to the worst-case scenario? Do you struggle with social anxiety or are you harder on yourself internally? Once you notice the main mental obstacles that keep you cycling through excessive mental chatter, it becomes easier to quiet those thoughts.

2. **Utilize a form of journaling to help you make better sense of your thoughts:** Whether you like digital journaling or physically writing things down, keep track of some of your emotions and challenge your day-to-day thought patterns. Utilize prompts to help you reflect on an even higher level.

3. **State neutral and positive affirmations to reduce the validity of negative affirmations:** Repetition is key, so even though they might be hard to believe at first, you can eventually get the hang of reminding yourself to start with natural affirmations.

These methods are realistic and everyday patterns that anyone can incorporate into their routine. At first, it might be hard to power through the mental chatter, but that's because it's become the main controlling factor in our mind. You might think to yourself that journaling or using positive affirmations is dumb or meaningless, but your brain might be conditioned to be pessimistic or lacking motivation to overcome the very thoughts that keep it held back. While it might feel uncomfortable to raise mental awareness in the beginning, remember to stay neutral and objective when analyzing thought patterns.

The voice that lingers in our minds is like a song that gets stuck in our heads. We might think we know all the words, but it's usually just a verse that repeats itself. You might think your worst thoughts are true, but once you start to investigate them and seek evidence, you will realize you know less than you thought. Fill in your mental blanks with validating and objective statements to serve as a reminder of just how valued, unique, and important you are.

Chapter 3:

Challenging Your Thoughts Through Neuroplasticity

When struggling with overthinking, it can feel like we are stuck with the brain we've been given. Fortunately enough, this isn't always the case! Our brains are plastic, meaning they can change shape over time, a reminder that rewiring negative thoughts is possible.

Have you ever walked a path through the woods or a hiking trail? Have you ever taken a shortcut across a grassy plain? Perhaps you followed a path that had been naturally dug into the soil through footprints over time. The more people that walk down that path, the deeper and more defined the path becomes. This is sometimes referred to as a "Desire Path." As people or animals continue over a path, it becomes more intense. Think of a path through the snow. The first time someone walks through fresh snow, it's difficult. As each person keeps going over the path, the snow eventually melts away. The 10th or 20th person to walk down the path has a much easier time than the first, and they likely walk down the trail without giving it much thought.

Our brain has similar pathways. Each time we learn something new, a pathway is created to help connect ideas and make sense of our surroundings. The more we walk down the path, the more likely we are to understand and remember that information. For example, when you first learn someone's name, your brain creates a record of that name. If this is a person you keep talking to daily, like a new coworker or romantic partner, then chances are, you'll remember their name much easier as that neural pathway is strengthened. However, if you only meet this person once, like a server at a restaurant or a first date you never see again, you won't strengthen that connection, and eventually, that information will fade away.

This example helps us to understand the plasticity of our brains. They are malleable, meaning we can shape them in different ways. The more that we go over the same information, the more likely we are to follow down those neural pathways.

When these pathways keep leading us to overthink, then it's more likely to become the default, leaving us struggling with our thoughts and dealing with excessive overthinking. It becomes natural to make negative assumptions or have intense fears when those are the strongest connections in our brains.

Now it's time for you to venture into uncharted territory. Explore new parts of your brain and create Desire Paths in areas you haven't walked before.

Connect Both Sides of Your Brain

We have two parts of our brain, and it's split in half between two hemispheres. The left and right sides work together to help us function from how we think to the way we act. The right side is more responsible for things like creativity, whereas the left side is more responsible for logical thinking. You can remember this by using this phrase: **L**eft equals **L**ogic, **R**ight equals c**R**eativity.

Some of us have one side of the brain that is a little stronger than the other. When we think more creatively, we might see problems and solutions much differently than somebody who thinks more logically. This can also determine how we explore the world. Some people can be spiritual and aren't interested in figuring out the more logical aspects of life. Others are more analytical and mathematical, and they need real answers and solutions.

Regardless of what individual you might be, one thing that can help us connect our minds to our bodies to reduce overthinking is to connect both sides of our brains. This is helpful because when we connect the right and left sides of our brain, it increases our coordination. It also makes it easier to kind of go with the flow and act on positive impulses.

When we are in line with our mind and body, it makes it easier to complete tasks and put our best foot forward, increasing productivity, and therefore output. One of the best ways for you to connect to the right and left sides of your brain is your alternate nostril breathing.

To do this, make a fist with your dominant hand. Now, stick out your thumb and then stick out your pinky at the same time. Keep your fist loose—it doesn't necessarily have to be a tight fist. It's just a way to help you stick out your pinky and your thumb. Then, place your thumb on your right nostril and close it. Breathe in through your left nostril as you count to five. Next, place your pinky on your left nostril, close it, and breathe out through your right nostril.

While your left nostril is still closed, breathe in through your right. Press it down with your thumb again and breathe out through your left. Keep repeating this back and forth as you count to five for a few sessions. If you feel lightheaded or dizzy, you can stop momentarily and breathe regularly. Once you've done this at least five times, then switch up your hands and repeat the process with your other hand. This is a great method that helps instantly pull your focus from mental chatter to the present moment.

Another powerful way to connect both sides of your brain is by using the opposite hand and changing up small routines. For example, if you're right-handed, chances are you brush your teeth with your right hand every night. For the next few nights, switch it up and brush your teeth with your left hand. Do this for eating as well. You likely eat using a fork with your right hand if you're right-handed, so try switching to your left hand. It might be a little uncomfortable at first, but after a while, you'll notice that it gets easier.

You can even challenge yourself to do things like writing with your non-dominant hand. Even doing something like taking the stairs can be done with our dominant side. You might take the first step with your right foot if you are right-handed. Change it up and take it with your left foot or vice versa if your left side is your more dominant side.

Pay attention throughout the day to notice which hand is more likely to lead and do your best to switch it up to keep challenging your mindset.

Writing in New Ways

Overcoming excessive mental chatter doesn't require a new brain; it simply requires that we start to think in brand-new ways. Reframing is one of the most powerful ways for us to gain a new perspective and have more power over our thoughts. Reframing can help you begin the process of not only reducing mental chatter in the first place but also making it less influential over your beliefs and actions.

Whenever we believe something, whether it's a basic thought we have or a value that's developed over time, it's easy to let this thing control our actions. For example, if you believe that people are generally not good and that others are out to get you, you might be more likely to be socially isolated. If you believe that other people are very judgmental or self-centered, you might not want to do things like interact with big groups or even date other people. However, social isolation can be very damaging to your mental and even physical health, therefore, it's important to overcome a belief like this. That is where reframing comes in.

It's okay if you're generally an introvert or somebody who likes to spend more time alone. However, it's important to do so because that's simply what you prefer and not based on any belief that the world is filled with evil people. Reframing our thoughts is a way that we can take some of the mental chatter that's been holding us back and actually transform it into something more productive and valuable to our overall perspective.

The first method of reframing is to start writing down your thoughts and experiences in the third person. This can be helpful because it gives us a bird's eye view of our situation. When we're in the middle of our problems and biggest conflicts, it's easy to only see things from our own personal perspective. However, when we take a step back from this situation and look at it through another person's lens, we gain new insight into some of the main issues that we've been dealing with. For example, if you're fighting with your partner, it's easy to let resentments and conflict intertwine with everything you've been experiencing. After a while, you start to build up more and more anger toward them, and it can be hard to see their point of view.

Rather than listening to the real issues to help you get to a resolution, you might be focused on defending yourself and trying to get what you want. Taking a step back and viewing the situation from the third-person perspective will help you see their point of view as well. To do this, first, start by writing out your situation in a story form. You might say something like, "Person A is struggling with their emotions, and Person B is struggling to understand what the other person is feeling."

Picture yourself as the narrator of your own story. Consider what your situation might look like if it were a movie script: What is the setting? Who are the characters? What driving forces are creating the motivations for the characters?

Another great perspective that can help you gain a better understanding is to step outside of your home and pretend like you're looking inside through the window. What do you physically and visually see in front of you? Start with the basic outline of the situation from a different perspective. This will help you alleviate some of the intense anxiety and panic that comes along as well.

For example, when you're in the middle of a financial crisis and struggling with bills or making money, it can feel like the end of the world when you are the one who is at the center of it. However, if you were looking through your neighbor's window and saw their stress while they opened utility bills, it might not seem as bad as it feels for that person. This can help us gain a new perspective on the situation. When some of the intense emotions are alleviated from the most chaotic situation that you find yourself in, it helps reduce some of the severity, therefore, making it easier to find realistic, practical, and concrete solutions.

Another method to help you reframe your situation is through the use of a character or persona for your thoughts. This means creating somebody who is the voice of your most negative or debilitating mental chatter. For example, you might name your negative voice "Chatty Cathy." Cathy is always going on about the worst-case scenario. She's always in there, nagging your brain, holding you back, and making you feel as though you are not good enough. When Chatty Cathy won't seem to shut up, what you can do is ask her to physically leave your mind. You can visualize yourself kicking her out, silencing her, or turning up the volume on something else to help drown out the sound of her voice.

When we create a character for our thoughts, it's easier to, literally, kick them out of our mind, therefore reducing some of that mental chatter. Chatty Cathy might keep trying to crawl her way back in, but you can still separate yourself from some of these debilitating thoughts by pushing her out.

Although it can seem counterintuitive for somebody experiencing anxiety, envisioning the worst-case scenario can also help push through mental chatter. This involves identifying what the least favorable outcome would be. The important thing is to stay realistic if you choose to use this method. For example, you might be going on a plane ride and you're worried because you feel as though you're going to get in a plane crash. This is very unrealistic. In reality, the worst case that might happen is that you miss your flight, or you have to sit next to a rude passenger.

Realistically, and statistically speaking, plane crashes are not that common, so it can help provide alleviation and a reminder that everything is likely going to be okay. If you are behind on your bills and you're struggling to keep up with everything, you might start picturing yourself losing your home or getting evicted and becoming homeless. You might see yourself 10 years from now with nothing to your name. However, realistically, the worst that's going to happen is you might get charged a late fee for missing a payment or perhaps it impacts your credit score. Realistically speaking, it's going to take a lot for you to lose everything you have, so remember to stay grounded when these negative situations arise and remind yourself that even if the worst-case scenario does happen, it's not the end of the world.

Using these different perspective changes can help you push through some of that mental chatter so that you can focus on what matters most and leave the rest behind.

Tap Into Your Senses

Sensory immersion is an important way for us to become more focused in the present moment. Our senses are the way that we can connect to the world around us. They are how we interpret things and can contribute to many different memories. They can help us find a deeper understanding and meaning behind the things that we experience on a day-to-day basis.

Any activity that absorbs your senses makes it easier for you to connect to the world and the task in front of you. For example, think of the last time you watched a really good movie. Perhaps you saw it in theaters. Chances are, it was the sights and noises that made you feel as though you were in the movie yourself. When was the last time you had a delicious meal? The textures, tastes, and smells of this meal might have pulled your focus in, helping distract you from the stressors of the world around you.

One of the most popular mindfulness activities that many people try is the five senses activity. To do this, you identify five things that you can see, four things you can touch, three things you can hear, two things you can smell, and one thing you can taste. You can do this activity no matter where you are. For example, let's say you are riding the train on your commute to work. Identify five things you see. This might be the person across from you. Perhaps one is a newspaper somebody's reading. You see somebody's red shoes. You see the map of the train station, and you see your reflection in the window. Next, identify four things you can feel. You feel the cold air coming out of the vent. You feel the plastic seat beneath you. You feel the hard ground, and you feel the cold metal poles as you're holding onto them during the bumpy train ride.

There are many things you can hear as well. Pick three of them. You hear the sound of the train. You hear somebody's music playing from their earbuds, and you hear somebody coughing on the other end of the train. There are plenty of smells within the subway station. You might smell somebody's perfume that they just sprayed or maybe you smell the natural stench of the train. Lastly, you can likely find something that you can taste. You don't have to actually taste this thing that you identify. For example, you might see somebody's coffee that they're holding. You don't have to go up and taste the coffee, but you can imagine what it tastes like yourself as you've likely had a sip of coffee in the past.

This sensory activity is a great way to help you stay more grounded and focused in the present moment. You can practice it in multiple different ways, and even after you identify all of your five senses in one area, you can challenge yourself to find even more. Start practicing this more when you are home alone and even when you are already in a good mood or feeling focused. This will make it more natural for you to start identifying your senses, even in times when you might not need the distraction as much.

Another great sensory activity is to shower in the dark. Of course, you should safely do this. However, this activity is a great method that you can utilize when you want to really feel your senses and pay attention to the bodily sensations that you're experiencing. Showering is a very common activity that many of us participate in without thinking twice. When you start to focus on all the senses that come along with a shower, it makes it easier to pull your focus in and explore the different physical feelings as they occur.

Next, holding a raisin is another great way to tap into your five senses. Hold the raisin in your hand and consider the texture that it has. Think about the way that it tastes, smells, and what it looks like. You can also use different objects as you're holding them to help you be more mindful. For example, consider a grape versus a raisin or a raisin versus something hard like a penny. Run your fingers over this small object and be extremely mindful of all the different ways that it interacts with your bodily sensations.

Try utilizing more five senses activities in the future. Consider trying a blind taste or smell test. Purchase your favorite beverage in three different ways. For example, if you really like lemon-lime soda, purchase three different brands of lemon-lime soda. Alternatively, purchase the same brand, just in different containers, like a plastic bottle, a can, or a glass bottle. Then, pour one into 3 different glasses, mixing them up so you don't know which is which. You can place a sticker or piece of tape on the bottom so you can check to see if you were correct after tasting each. You can also do this with a partner to help you keep track of the different flavors.

Participating in these mindful activities regularly can help you explore some of the deepest parts of sensory immersion. Once you connect your mind to your body, it helps pull you into the world around you, therefore reducing the mental chatter. It's always best to stay in the present moment rather than fixating on the past or worrying about the future when overcoming overthinking.

Chapter Review

You only have one brain, but the good news is, it can be changed! While many foundational aspects will remain, how our brain thinks can be altered over time. You can't change experiences, but you can look at them with a new perspective. You can't predict what will happen in the future, but you can remind yourself that you are going to be okay no matter what.

It's also important to remember that there is a very strong connection between our minds and bodies. Even the most intelligent scientists still don't understand everything there is to know about the human brain, but that's okay! We don't have to know everything to help us make the most of our powerful neurological system.

Remember to utilize these ways to tap into your mind's potential:

1. **Connect the right and left sides of your brain:** Bring them together to form one, cohesive mindset to make the most of your mental power. When our body is out of order and we

don't feel physically connected, that can show in the way we think, feel, and act.

2. **Shift perspectives and see things from a new lens:** Open your mind to new potentials and consider things you haven't before. When you start challenging your mind to explore areas you haven't before, you will be flooded with epiphanies and realizations that can bring clarity to the mental chatter that causes confusion and disorientation.

3. **We have five senses, so learn how to use them in everything you do!** When you create normalcy around utilizing all of these senses, it will make it easier to stay grounded and mindful in each moment.

The mind and body are two parts of us that must become connected if we want to maintain total control over what's going on inside of our heads. We are imperfect beings, and once we learn to embrace every part of ourselves, we will become more comfortable with that imperfection. This allows us to embrace our thoughts rather than feeling stifled by them. Both mental and spatial awareness are grown when we focus on how our minds connect to our bodies.

As mindfulness becomes more familiar to you, it will then become easier to add it into daily life.

Chapter 4:

Incorporating Mindfulness into Daily Life

When you arise in the morning, think of what a privilege it is to be alive, to think, to enjoy, to love... —Marcus Aurelius

Mindfulness isn't just a habit to practice when you're anxious or struggling with overthinking. Mindfulness is a tool that can help us become more appreciative and present in our daily lives. Take something as simple as a flower. We probably see at least a flower every single day, if not more. Such a ubiquitous symbol can fade into the background, and as we see more and more, we might begin to lose appreciation for this natural creation. But imagine watching a flower grow from seed into a blossoming, colorful pedal.

Seeing every stage of growth is inspiring and serves as a reminder of the preciousness of nature. If you were to study a flower for 10 minutes or more, you would start to notice more details. You might see the veins or patterns on the stalks and petals. Other activities can help you increase this mindfulness and take it to an even bigger level. If you had to draw the flower, for example, you would notice things you wouldn't have otherwise.

As we go throughout our daily lives, we repeat the same habits. We go through the same motions and do the same things. Showering is a way to get clean. Eating is a way to silence our rumbling stomachs. Cleaning is a way to power through our chores. However, if we learn to utilize mindfulness, we can turn the mundane into a miracle. By opening your eyes to the beauty in the world around you, you can begin to see things in brand new ways like you never would have otherwise.

Mindfulness isn't something to use only when you can't breathe or feel like you're dying. If you learn how to be mindful even in the happy moments, you appreciate them more. You can strengthen your memory and notice small things that others neglect. You will also find that it becomes even easier to use mindfulness in those moments of overthinking when you make it a natural part of your everyday life.

Learning to Mindfully Eat

Eating is something that we have to do every day, multiple times a day. Because of the routine nature of eating, it's easy to start to eat more mindlessly. However, when we lose track of our eating habits, this can result in binge eating or overeating, which can also perpetuate even more unhealthy eating habits. Eating is a great way to help keep us mindful, especially since it's an activity we do multiple times throughout the day. What does it mean to eat mindlessly? Eating mindlessly is something like grabbing an entire bag of chips and eating it without keeping track of your portions.

Mindless eating also involves eating meals in front of the TV while watching a movie or your favorite show. While this can be a fun activity, it can lead to habits where eventually you *have* to sit in front of the TV when you're eating or else you find it to be less enjoyable. Mindful eating is when we pay more attention to what we're doing and all of the sensations that come along with eating.

Mindless eating involves eating food without paying attention. This might also include eating quickly. If you grab food on your way to work or during a commute, you might eat it as quickly as possible without enjoying the sensation. Everyone has to eat a quick meal once in a while, especially because of our busy schedules. But if this becomes a daily habit, it can lead to unhealthy eating habits.

Mindful eating is when you are more engaged with the act of eating and it can help increase your presence in the moment. It also helps you listen to your bodily cues more. For example, mindless eating would be eating an entire package of cookies or bag of chips whereas mindful eating would allow you to take just a handful and eat a small amount at a time. If you end up still being hungry after, you can grab more. However, you'll find that most of the time, a handful of food is satisfying enough. This will help you control over-eating, which can lead to even more healthier choices later on in life.

Eating more mindfully can help you enjoy this experience more as well. To eat more mindfully, start by eliminating distractions. This involves eating at a table and sitting down with your family rather than sitting in front of the TV. This also requires that we eat on plates and serve out portions, enabling us to eat a specific amount. If you want to eat some chips, pour them into a bowl rather than eating straight from the bag. If you get takeout from a restaurant, portion it out and place it on your plate rather than eating directly from the box or container.

As you are eating, chew your food as many times as possible. Savor it in your mouth and let it sit momentarily as you absorb all the flavors. Try to identify two or three flavors in everything that you're eating. For example, if you're eating something as simple as a slice of pizza, you might chomp it down quickly. When eating mindfully, take one bite at a time. Identify different flavors. What does the bread taste like? What does the cheese taste like? Can you identify any toppings in the piece that you just took a bite out of? Swallow it slowly and wait a moment before moving on to the next bite.

You can also increase mindful eating in times outside of just the act of consuming meals by practicing specific mindful eating exercises. For example, pick something simple and whole, like a fruit or vegetable. What is your favorite fruit? This might be an apple or a strawberry. Sit at a table without any distractions and take one bite as slowly as you can. Savor each bite and pay attention to the way that your entire body feels as you're consuming this food. Another great way to mindfully eat is to take something whole like a fruit or vegetable and cut it into different-sized pieces and shapes. For example, if you have something like a banana, you can cut it into small discs, or you can cut it into long strips. This will help you recognize the way that different shapes and textures can contribute to flavor overall.

Eat something with utensils that you normally wouldn't. For example, get your favorite chip and use chopsticks or a fork to try to eat this rather than using your hands. Alternatively, use something that you need to eat with a utensil and use your hands, like spaghetti. It can be a messy activity, but it can help you understand the way that you automatically eat and raise awareness of some of those thoughtless habits that you might have when consuming different foods.

The more that you practice mindful eating, the easier it will be to stay present in the moment and develop healthy eating habits. This can not only help your overall nutrition, but it can also make you more present throughout the day, therefore helping to reduce mental chatter.

Change Up Your Space

Our thoughts are influenced by our environment and that includes the things that physically fill our environment, such as furniture decorations, and clutter. Our space is filled with an endless amount of triggers. Seeing these triggers can then lead to a stream of thoughts that could either be very beneficial and productive, or they can be very distracting and hold you back.

We must start recognizing the space around us because things like physical clutter can often lead to mental clutter. Anything you see could trigger an emotion, a feeling, a thought, or a memory. It might drive you to take action and lead you to feel a certain way. If we're not careful or aware of how this is impacting our mindset, then it could be potentially damaging to our day-to-day thought patterns. For example, let's say your office space is a collection of clutter. You have stacks of unopened mail, piles of unread books, and half-finished projects in every single corner.

What this will do is distract from work. You'll see the unopened mail and you'll think about all the potentially stressful things that await inside each letter. Is it a utility bill that is too expensive to pay or a notice from the IRS letting you know that you owe them taxes? When you see piles of unfinished books, you might start to think about how you need to read more and it will trigger you to think about the content that might be inside the books. When you see half-finished projects lying around, you might feel defeated or like you're not successful or productive enough.

All of these can contribute to negative feelings and emotions, therefore making it harder to focus on work going forward. When your space is disorganized or chaotic, then that will be a reflection of how your thought processes might be. It can be very damaging to your cognitive function, therefore making it hard to push through mental chatter.

Chaotic or messy spaces can be very overstimulating to the mind and anything around you that starts to distract you is something that takes away from your ability to get work done. research shows that clutter (Sander, 2019):

- increases anxiety
- disrupts sleep
- reduces focus
- increases impulsive behavior
- impacts relationships

To help you make the most of your space around you, it's important to pay attention to the way that it makes you feel now. Do you feel safe, organized, and focused in your spaces? Or do you feel overwhelmed? Do you feel bombarded with decisions or fatigued by the endless stimulation?

If so, it's time to change up your space. This means first decluttering. Go through things that you no longer need and get rid of them. Learn to let things go. It can be hard to do so because what if we end up needing this thing later on or what if it becomes valuable later in life? The endless "what ifs" can be overwhelming.

It's important to remember that anything valuable to you now is something that you're likely using consistently. If something holds memories and you don't want to let it go for nostalgic reasons, take a picture of it and create a photo album of all the things that you didn't want to have to physically let go of. This way, you can still look at that item and remember it fondly without having to keep it in your home where it's taking up excessive space.

At the same time, it's also good to remember that you can hold onto things and simply move them out of your line of vision. Invest in some plastic bins to help you store things away. While you might still have excessive clutter or things to go through, at least getting them out of your visual field can help reduce the impact that they might have on your cognitive function.

You can also keep a temporary declutter bin. What this means is putting away things that you think you don't need, but you're too afraid to let go of yet. Then in three months, six months, or a year, check back in with this bin. Is there anything that you could have let go that you forgot you were holding on to? Or is there something that you're happy that you kept? This will help you gain a better insight into what is valuable, what should be kept, and what is okay to finally let go of.

Lastly, it's important to remember that even if your space is seemingly clutter-free or organized, changing things up is a great way to help change up your mindset. It's kind of like getting a new haircut or a new wardrobe. It's a way to refresh and reset the space around you so that you can start thinking in new ways. We are creatures of habit and that routine nature within us can lead us to think in similar ways, even when we try hard to break old mental patterns. If you want to move forward into a life of reducing mental chatter, it can be very helpful to start the process of giving your space a makeover. Paint a wall a new color or buy yourself a new desk or couch.

Change the direction that your living room faces or move your bed to a different wall. These small changes can be very impactful in altering the way that we think or feel. When you have a new space, you might have a new mindset, making it easier to stay one step ahead of the mental clutter.

Chunk Tasks and Time Yourself

One of the biggest disadvantages of mental clutter is just how distracting it can be. It can keep us from being productive and getting things done. It keeps us trapped in our heads rather than in the present moment where we can focus and be more productive individuals. The process of combating mental clutter can be difficult when you are struggling to recognize the negative impact of that excessive mental chatter.

When we overthink, it is very easy to get distracted. This can then lead to procrastination. When we are chronically procrastinating, we might begin to overthink our work and question our abilities. Eventually, procrastination can even lead to bigger issues like perfectionism. Perfectionism is another thing that perpetuates all-or-nothing patterns of thought.

As you can see, mental chatter can easily become a cycle of avoidance tendencies on top of subpar work. The solution to procrastination and overcoming distracting mental chatter is by increasing our productivity. The first way to do this is to break tasks down into smaller milestones. If you want to climb a mountain, you have to start with the first step. When you stand back and look at the entirety of the mountain, it can be very overwhelming and daunting. You wonder if you're going to be able to do it. You start thinking about all the ways that you might trip and fall down the mountain. You think about how tired you're going to be. However, if you simply take it one step at a time, before you know it, you're halfway there.

Break large tasks into the smallest, most manageable size possible. This means if you need to clean your entire kitchen, list out all the small steps involved. Begin by picking up the trash or garbage. Next, you want to wash things like dirty dishes. After that, you can do some organization and other forms of basic cleaning. By breaking big tasks down into 10 different tasks, you can knock things out one at a time, therefore making it easier to work through these milestones.

Once you start knocking things off your to-do list, it then provides you with a greater sense of accomplishment and serves as a reminder that you are capable of getting things started when you put your mind to it. This provides you with even more motivation to keep working on things, which will help you power through the mental chatter.

When you break tasks down, you're also increasing mindfulness because you're identifying all the realistic steps that are involved. When we try to do one big thing at a time, it's easy to get overwhelmed with all the what-if scenarios.

However, when you have small and more manageable pieces, it's therefore easier to realistically see that you're capable of achieving all of these little parts. Once you knock milestones off your to-do list, it's important to celebrate. Celebrating increases positivity and boosts your motivational mindset. It's your way of recognizing your abilities and reminding yourself that you're deserving of celebration and happiness because of your hard work and effort. It's a way that you can recognize just how productive you've been and also acknowledge the sacrifices that you made to get there.

This is all forms of positive reinforcement, therefore making you more likely to be productive again in the future. Celebrations don't have to be expensive or elaborate. They can be something like eating your favorite snack or watching an episode of your favorite show in between tasks.

Another important method to help push through mental chatter is through the use of timing yourself. When you give yourself a time limit, you have an actual countdown that you can look at, therefore making you more likely to stay focused on the present moment as you see the clock ticking away. You will remind yourself that you need to keep pushing forward and you need to keep focusing so that you don't get distracted by other tasks. It also helps ensure that you ring in any perfectionist tendencies. Sometimes when we get focused on a task, it's easy to think about all the ways that we could improve. You might want to start things over again or redo the work that you've already finished. However, this can lead to even more overthinking and distraction. The timer keeps you focused and helps you realize that it's better to just get something done than to continue to avoid a task because ultimately, you'll end up getting nothing done.

By combining these different types of strategies, you enable yourself to power through some of the mental chatter. It's also helpful to chunk big tasks together so that you can organize all those small milestones. For example, if you're cleaning the house, your first thought might be to go room by room and finish these one at a time. However, chunk similar tasks together first. This might mean going through and picking up all the garbage or trash. Next, you can do all the deep cleaning things like dusting or wiping off surfaces. Lastly, you can do all the floors of the entire house. If you chunk similar tasks, then you might find it easier to be more productive and knock things out much quicker. Utilizing these strategies is a great way to ensure that you stay focused on what requires your attention the most at the present moment.

Chapter Review

Life passes by quickly and it doesn't ever stop. Even when something stressful or life-altering finds its way into our timeline, the sun keeps setting and the wind keeps blowing. If we don't learn to slow down and enjoy each moment that passes, we will lose more than just time.

Being present isn't just to avoid stress and anxiety but to help us make the moment of each day that we have here. There's no telling what tomorrow brings, and while there are plenty of things that cause us stress and anxiety, there is so much left to cherish. Remember to use different ways to incorporate mindfulness into daily life, like:

1. **Eat mindfully:** Enjoy each flavor or sensation that you consume. Pay attention to different flavor notes and notice the richness behind culinary dishes. Explore new foods and textures, even if you thought you didn't like them before.

2. **Create a mindful space:** Some of our belongings can blend in with the scenery over time, but it's important to pay attention to how they affect our thought processes. From the color of

the walls to the clutter on your desk, notice the way your surroundings might be adding to mental chatter.

3. **Be mindful of your time:** Time is fluid, but we can add structure to it to help us stay in line. When we are productive, we can overcome procrastination and other avoidance tendencies. When we get things done, it boosts our confidence and makes us feel better about ourselves, contributing to a happier mood overall.

Right now, mental chatter is likely a regular part of your routine, but that doesn't have to be the way things are forever! Going forward, you can utilize mindfulness in every area of your life, meaning that presence and awareness come more naturally to you rather than stress and panic. Can you imagine that life? While it might seem far-fetched, it's consistency that is key to achieving this.

The great thing about this type of mindfulness is that it can eventually spread to others as well, making those you love the most just as mindful and present as you are. When an entire group can enjoy each moment that passes, it can make life that much more enjoyable.

Chapter 5:

Group Mindfulness and Activities for Everyone

Humans are adaptive, intelligent, and creative individuals. But when we put them into a group, magic happens. We come up with solutions, learn from each other, and take on one another in ways that we couldn't on our own.

Socialization is an important part of daily life for both survival and entertainment purposes. We rely on other people to provide us with basic necessities. Sure, you can go to the store and purchase your own ingredients for dinner, but who was it that brought those ingredients to the store? Who farmed the animals and plants that you want to eat? Who built the coolers and trucks that keep this food safe?

Our social groups might be small, but society is big. The idea of living within groups isn't just a concept humans utilize. Primates and other animals also function within small groups. In fact, some primate communities include as many as 150 members (Chapman & Teichroeb, 2012). Survival isn't easy, and we need to rely on others for a multitude of reasons. Beyond this, communities help ensure we gain a sense of fulfillment. Consider social activities like playing games, laughing, watching TV, dancing, and even kissing and hugging. These provide us with warmth, comfort, and security.

Other people make us feel good, and a lack of socialization can have a negative impact on our health. Social isolation can cause mental illness, cognitive decline, and a weakened immune system (Novotney, 2019). Mindfulness can be used to not only increase the amount of socialization you receive but also help strengthen social interactions to make the most of them.

Finding a way to incorporate mindfulness at work, with your family, or in your social circle will make it easier to incorporate mindfulness into daily life.

Bodily Synchronization

Now that we've discussed some of the methods of increasing your mental awareness, we can finally move on to how to increase social awareness. It's easy to first start becoming more aware mentally and internally because it only requires ourselves. However, now it's time to apply that to the world around us. From your spouse to the barista at the coffee shop down the block, you can increase your presence in social situations to help make the most of them.

One way to do this is through bodily synchronization. This involves raising awareness over body language. When we get stuck in our heads and struggle with overthinking, it's easy to assume the worst about other people. We assume that they're judging us or that they are focused on our flaws. However, once you start to raise your social awareness, you realize that people are much more focused on themselves than they are on you. Raising mindfulness in the present moment can be done through body language. This first begins by noticing the way that you are holding your body in social situations. We express our thoughts through what we say but just as expressive can be our body language.

This begins with something like our facial expressions. You have so many muscles in your face. These help show when you are happy, surprised, upset, disgusted, repulsed, intrigued, curious, angry, frustrated, and so on. There are a multitude of different emotional ways that we show exactly what's going on in our minds. Have you ever been able to tell what somebody was thinking without them saying a single word? You might have simply known their facial expressions well enough.

To help you gain a better understanding of how you express your emotions through your facial expressions, take a moment and stand in front of a mirror. Try making different facial expressions like anger, frustration, curiosity, repulsion, happiness, or surprise. Then consider how you might show this to different people. How would you show anger to the person that you feel closest with versus somebody that you don't know that well? How might you show love or romance to your long-term partner versus somebody you're going on a first date with? Challenge yourself to try out different facial expressions so you can get a better understanding of what other people are seeing when they have conversations with you.

Aside from facial expressions, how we hold our bodies can be very telling of what's going on in our minds. Right now, take a moment to roll your shoulders back and sit up straight, stretch your legs out, and sit in a comfortable position. What you might find is that the way that your body changes can also change the way that your mind is thinking. When in social settings, we could express different things like anxiety or comfort based on the way that we're holding our bodies. If you have your arms and legs spread open and relaxed, it shows that you're comfortable in the moment.

If you are very closed off and experiencing tight muscles, then it can show that you might be experiencing more discomfort. Once you raise awareness of your body language, you can then start to apply that to how you interpret what another person is feeling. Do they have their arms crossed? Do they have their brows furrowed? Do they have their heads tilted? Do they have their arms open? All these intricacies of how somebody is using their body can be very telling of what might be going on inside their head.

By learning different language cues from other people and noticing what might be going on in their heads, we can connect to others more physically. If you notice that somebody is feeling anxious and uncomfortable, you might change the subject or ask how they're feeling. If somebody is closed off and struggling to open up, perhaps you can hand them something, such as a drink, to help them calm down. If somebody is starting to feel angry or defensive, you might lighten your tone and redirect the conversation more productively.

Perhaps you can do things like turn on some music or change the lighting to help make people more comfortable if they seem as though they're closed off and anxious. Reading body language is a practice that can take time to master, but by increasing your spatial and social awareness, you'll be able to connect with others and be more present in the moment as you are socializing.

Use Weekly Mindfulness

Mindfulness is something that we can bring home to the whole family to help increase the presence of everyone involved. Whether you live with three roommates or you're married with kids, there are many different methods of mindfulness to incorporate to help increase presence and reduce mental chatter for all parties. When one person is mindful, it can spread to the next person, helping to make social interactions that much more enjoyable. This can also help your home life if you find that you are struggling with other people. For example, perhaps you and your partner are frequently fighting. Maybe it's because both of you have been focused on your own mindset rather than what's been going on in your personal life. Perhaps your kids are struggling to pay attention in school, or you find that you are becoming disconnected from other family members. Increasing mindfulness can help make the situation more comfortable so everybody can open up and express how they might be feeling.

One way to make mindfulness a more regular part of your life is to utilize it on a weekly basis. First and foremost, set a specific day to be mindful with your family. This might be doing something like having a game night every Monday or having a screen-free day every week. Game nights are great ways to make sure that everybody is present and focused. You could also invite other people over to participate in your game night. Choose things that require teamwork and logic-building skills to make sure that you and all parties involved are more aware as things are unfolding around you. This includes something like the game charades. Turn off the TV, and at the most, play some music in the background. Make some snacks to also encourage mindful eating, and consider making a fun drink for the whole family.

Screen-free days are also really beneficial for boosting mindfulness. This means everybody has to put their phone away. You can still have one close by in case of emergencies, but for the most part, there should be an emphasis on everyone turning their devices off and being present with one another. You don't always have to participate in an activity together either. The screen-free day could involve simply reading while in the same room as one another. Screen-free periods also help you realize just how addicted you might be to these different types of devices.

Another idea for increasing mindfulness in a social setting is through nature walks. These are great for everybody in the family. Going on a nature walk with your partner can help you connect to each other on a deeper level. You can discuss things that have been on your mind and share different thoughts and ideas. If you go with a whole family, you can make it into a fun game. Play something like I Spy where you have to pick out something that's a certain color. You could even do a scavenger hunt, where everybody has to find something that has a specific color or texture. Come up with the rules for the scavenger hunt with your family before getting started. Consider things like finding something made out of wood, finding a certain type of leaf, or picking out something that's a specific color.

Another great way to utilize weekly mindfulness is through a book or movie club. Books and movies are great ways for us to be more aware of the present moment and stay focused when we are with other people. Pick out a specific book to read by a certain time period. Take notes as you're reading the book so that you have material to discuss once you're with other people. After everyone has finished the book or finished up to a certain point, you can get together and start discussing some of the things that you have been reading.

Movies are also great ways to increase mindfulness, especially for those who might not be as interested in reading books. This involves picking out a movie to watch weekly with other people, getting together to watch it, and then after, discussing the movie. Have different themes for the books or movies, like different subjects or different authors. Take turns picking these books and movies to help increase engagement and make it more exciting for everybody involved. You could even do a combination book and movie club where you watch movies based on books.

Lastly, a great way to increase mindfulness at home is through the use of family gratitude. Gratitude is a powerful way for us to recognize the things that we have in life to be thankful for. Gratitude is not the dismissal of struggles or other negative things in our lives. It's simply the acknowledgment that no matter what might be going on, there are still things for us to be grateful for. Showing gratitude is something that you can do daily. Take turns stating one thing that you're grateful for each meal time, whether you do this during breakfast or at night during dinner.

Make sure that every member of your family states one thing that they are grateful for. This helps to bring awareness and mindfulness to the present moment, while also inspiring you for things to be grateful for that you might not have thought of had it not been for what another person said. Small things we can be grateful for are things like delicious meals, good movies, or laughing with friends and family. You could think of things on a larger scale, like being grateful for your health. The more that you practice it, the easier it will be to naturally think of things that you're grateful for, therefore, boosting your happiness and mindfulness in the presence of others.

Create Something Together

Creating something in a group can increase mindfulness. When we are creative, we have to generate ideas. It forces us to work together to come up with solutions and innovations we might not have thought of otherwise. When creating something in a group, you come together and use everyone’s strengths to work together to reach a common goal. When you are creative in a group setting, you also can learn new things from each other. For example, when cooking, you might find a new way to chop a vegetable or season a dish. Group creativity is a great way to ensure everyone’s attention is pulled to the same place, allowing everyone the ability to learn from each other and showcase their uniqueness.

Mindful meals can connect groups on a deeper level. Food is something that can connect us on so many levels. The tastes and smells create mental memories that we can return to in the future. It's easy to get triggered by sights and smells, instantly pulling us back to the time that we enjoyed the meal. Below are a few tips and ideas to help you make the most out of mindful group meals:

- **Cook a fancy meal:** Some meals are complex or require expensive ingredients. Getting together with other people can help make it easier to power through challenges while also sharing costs!

- **Have a potluck:** Consider hosting a potluck where everyone brings a different dish. Make it themed like everyone brings something that is a specific color, or all the dishes have to include a certain type of ingredient.

- **Partake in a competition:** Host a competition where everyone makes the same dish, and then everyone votes on whose is the best (with the only rule being that you can't vote for yourself). Ideas include things like chili, macaroni, and cheese, or chocolate chip cookies.

- **Decorate cookies:** Get together with friends or family and sit around a table as you all decorate cookies together. This is great for the holidays or special occasions, like a birthday. When you're done, everyone can enjoy the flavor and beauty of your creations!

- **Build a charcuterie:** A charcuterie board usually consists of cheese, crackers, and sliced meat, as well as vegetables, fruits, nuts, and dips. Consider hosting a charcuterie party, where everyone has to come together and bring an ingredient to create a board. It's exciting to see what everyone comes up with!

Mindful crafts are a great way to fill busy time and have something substantial to remember after. They require that everyone come together to work on the same goal. Some crafts can be done together in the sense that everyone is creating one thing, or everyone can create their version of a similar craft. Below are some ideas for group mindful crafts to try in a family or social circle:

- **Create a group quilt:** Invite friends over or have your family go through their closets and clean out old scraps of fabric or clothing they no longer need. Then, everyone can cut up these old pieces of clothing and swap different bits and pieces with one another. Afterward, use the scraps to create a unique quilt using these upcycled materials.

- **Paint pots for plants:** Head to your local hardware store and purchase several terra cotta planters. Then, get together with some friends or family members and paint the pots! After, you will always have something to admire and remind you of the time you spent together.

- **Create clay coasters:** Using air-dry clay, get together with others to create coasters. Everyone can create 4-5, and then swap them out with one another. This way you will have a set of completely unique coasters that remind you of those you spent time with.

- **Decorate birdhouses:** Using random bits of paper or other crafting scraps around the house, get together with friends to decorate birdhouses. If everyone brings over a few supplies, you will have a ton of options to choose from when decorating!

- **Tie-dye t-shirts:** Purchase some fabric dye and have everyone bring over 1-3 pieces of white clothing. Then spend some time together tying and dying these items. You will all have unique new outfits to wear that will remind you of each other.

Art extends beyond crafts and there are many other creative ways to connect and be mindful. Below are some ideas and inspirations for you and others to come together to strengthen your artistic skills and show one another a deeper side of the right side of your brain:

- **Make portraits of each other:** This is a great activity for small groups. Using your favorite medium (paint, pencils, pens, etc.), pick a partner to draw. Each of you can sit across from each other and sketch one another. It's exciting to see what everyone comes up with!

- **Write a story:** This is a fun game to play in a group. How it works is each person takes a turn saying one word that connects to the last, creating a fun story by the end. The words and phrases that come out of this game can be really funny, helping the group connect on many different levels.

- **Create a dance routine:** You don't have to be a professional dancer to create a dance routine! For this activity, get together with a group and pick out a song you all love. Then, based on your skill level, come up with a fun routine. It's also exciting to share it online with other friends and family!

- **Go see a live show:** Getting out into the world and participating in art with a group of friends is a great way to help you immerse yourself in the moment. Get tickets to a live orchestra or to see your favorite band with others.

- **Jam out:** Whether you play an instrument or you're an expert air guitarist, take some time to have fun with friends and jam out! If everyone brings an instrument, you can all try to learn a specific song or just play some notes and see what happens.

Mindful gardens are not only good for forming bonds, but they have benefits to the environment and potentially your grocery budget! Whether you want to grow an indoor plant or are planning a community garden, there are many benefits to starting a group garden. Below are some tips and tricks to help you get started:

- **Start seeds and share:** For this activity, have a few people you know purchase different seed packets. Then, everyone does their best to grow a few different small plants. Once the seeds are established, everyone can swap these small plants so you each have one! It's a great challenge to keep you mindful and focused on a daily basis.

- **Create a mosaic garden:** In your household, get together to create a beautiful mosaic garden. Each person can pick out a plant or flower of a different color. Then, get together to create a pattern or unique design using these in your backyard. When you're done, you'll have a beautiful garden that creates a unique mosaic.

- **Swap cuttings:** If you and other people you know already have some houseplants or an indoor garden, take some time to trim cuttings off of your plants. Then, swap these cuttings and plant them on your own. You will help your indoor garden grow while also having something to remind you of your loved ones.

- **Adopt a plant:** This method is great for those who don't have a green thumb. For this activity, go to your local garden store with some friends. Pick out a plant and split the cost. Then, take turns caring for the plant. Each week, give the plant to the next person, cycling through each other. This helps you stay connected while also giving the group a challenge: keep the plant alive!

- **Create a pollinator garden:** Whether you have a big yard or a small patio, you can create a garden to help give back to nature. A pollinator garden promotes insect life. Pick out several different flowers and plant them in an area where you can sit and watch. After, spend more time outside with your family as you notice bees, birds, and butterflies enjoy your creation.

Lastly, consider ways to mindfully volunteer. This provides groups with a sense of fulfillment while also giving back to the community. Some ideas of group mindfulness volunteer activities that can increase gratitude include running a food drive or helping out at an animal shelter. You can also purchase gifts and spend time wrapping them together to donate during the holidays.

There are plenty of fun and unique ways we can increase mindfulness in group settings. By doing this, you strengthen connections while also creating more meaningful memories with one another.

Chapter Review

Some of the best things in life include other people! Being able to connect to others is a great way to help us stay more mindful and make the most out of every interaction. It's not always easy! Sometimes you might feel very mindful when you are home alone, and then once you are around others, you forget everything you know about being present. When we make mindfulness a regular thing with others, we are more likely to be present when interacting.

Social isolation can have detrimental health effects, so we must learn how to be comfortable in the presence of everyone, from our closest loved ones to new people, we're meeting for the first time! There are plenty of bad people in the world, but most of the important individuals we interact with can provide us with a sense of fulfillment and happy memories. To increase mindfulness socially, remember to utilize these methods:

1. **Pay attention to body language:** You will notice so much about what a person is saying by *how* they say it rather than by focusing on just the words they choose to use. This can help you power through conflict to find a resolution. It can also serve as a reminder that most other people are going to be just as nervous as you are!

2. **Use regular mindfulness at home:** Whether you live with a roommate or your spouse and six kids, there are many ways you can incorporate mindfulness into your daily routine. From meals to entertainment, find small ways to utilize mindfulness to help your family make the most of their time together.

3. **Get creative in a group setting:** Learn from others and explore ideas you wouldn't have thought of if you were creating something on your own. Make memories with others and distract yourself with art. This will lessen the pressure of creating something new, therefore making it a more enjoyable process.

We only have one life to live, and that's a statement that is true for every single person we know. It's a human experience that we can relate to each other. By helping each other make the most of the moment, we can quiet mental chatter to get the things we want and connect with friends in unimaginable ways.

Chapter 6:

Reducing Overthinking and Increasing Your Health

Sometimes our thoughts run wild not because of just what's going on in our brains, but through the way that we're treating our bodies. Oftentimes, the chatter rises because of what we're doing to our body on a physical level. Stress and anxiety increase when we are not cautious of the four corners of health.

We exist inside a strong structure. Think of this structure like a car. Like a car, we require four wheels to keep us moving along. Each wheel plays an important part in ensuring there is a steady motion forward. Three of those wheels are enough to keep the car moving for a short period, but because of the extra added weight, they will eventually become weakened if one tire is removed.

To ensure we function properly, we need four wheels to keep us pushing forward. These four wheels represent the four parts of your health.

The four parts of health are:

- Mental health
- Sleep health
- Physical health
- Nutritional health

Together, these create a structure that helps us no matter what. There's a good chance that your mental health might be struggling if one of these other areas is also lacking. We only have so much energy and time that we can dedicate to our health, so we must focus on building up these four corners to reduce overthinking. Throughout most of the book, we've focused on our mental health, so let's take a look at some simple and realistic strategies you can use to boost mental health.

Fine Tune Your Food

There's a saying that you are what you eat, and that can be true, especially if you're somebody who struggles with mental chatter. If your eating habits are chaotic and disorganized and you don't pay a lot of attention to the foods that you choose to put in your body, then chances are, they might be impacting the way that your brain functions.

Our brain is the most important part of our body. That means it's going to get fed first, above all else. Other organs like your heart, lungs, and stomach are important to your overall function, but without the brain, none of those things would be able to operate properly. This means that what we eat is responsible for energizing our brain before anything else.

If you're struggling with brain fog, or you feel like you have bursts of energy and then end up feeling tired later on, it could be because you're not giving your brain healthy, nutritious foods that energize it in the best way possible. For example, one food that can travel quickly through our brains is sugar. Sugar is incredibly necessary for survival; it's found in many of the foods that we eat naturally. However, added sugar can be very impactful on our overall health and well-being. Processed sugar can be found in food like soda, candy, and even seemingly savory or healthy foods like pasta sauce or salad dressing. The sugar that is found in many processed foods like this energizes the brain, but it doesn't sustain it for a long period of time. You might find yourself feeling energetic and hyper after eating sugary foods, but eventually, you end up crashing pretty hard and it becomes difficult to focus.

Consider how you might eat sugar when you first wake up. Many breakfast foods like pastries, cereal, muffins, or donuts are advertised and sold to us under the guise that they create whole breakfasts. However, this added to sugary coffee drinks or energy drinks is loaded with sugar that fills us up but doesn't sustain us throughout the day. While it might seem like a caramel iced coffee and muffin are a small, harmless breakfast, if that's all you're eating, it could be contributing to brain fog throughout the day.

You don't have to give up on these foods altogether, and there's no shame in enjoying them. Our society already does a good job of shaming our dietary habits, so that's not what I'm here to do. However, I do want you to start considering the foods that you're eating and whether or not they're sustaining long-term, whole health. Enjoy that sweet coffee and morning donut, but add in a slice of avocado toast or green smoothie to ensure you're getting proper nutrition.

Nutrition plays a vital role in maintaining our overall well-being, both physically and mentally. Eating nutritious foods and following a balanced diet isn't just about having a certain body or looking a specific way. It's all about making sure that you are optimally functioning and maintaining high energy levels to keep you motivated and focused in the present moment. When you're constantly eating foods that aren't sustaining you throughout the day, you might feel really tired and lethargic. You might find yourself struggling to get things done or stay productive. This can eventually lead to anxiety, disappointment, and a lack of motivation which could also contribute to depressive episodes. Before you know it, the foods that you're choosing to eat are contributing to poor mental health, making it even harder to overcome overthinking.

It's also important to note foods that might be increasing our stress. For example, something like caffeine can make us really energetic. Many of us depend on it for the morning, and we might even enjoy it throughout the day. If you're somebody who is drinking three or more coffees, energy drinks, or caffeine-filled sodas throughout the day, you might find yourself feeling shaky and jittery. Even if you are consuming sugar-free coffee or diet soda, you can still struggle with some of the effects of excessive caffeine. Again, caffeine is not something to be demonized and you don't have to give it up altogether. But if you find yourself stuck with mental chatter, consider the caffeine levels that you are consuming on a daily basis.

To be free from mental chatter, you don't have to wipe everything out of your diet that you love and enjoy. You don't have to starve yourself or deprive yourself of things that make you happy. It's important that we limit things that aren't sustaining our nutrition and that we fill in the holes with healthier options.

One place to start is by incorporating fiber-rich foods and whole grains, as these can help sustain your energy levels throughout the day. This means eating whole foods, like fruits and vegetables, such as apples, bananas, spinach, and other greens. It's also important to choose lean meats as these are packed with protein that makes you feel full for longer periods of time. Consider fatty fish that are rich in omega-3 fatty acids, such as salmon, tuna, or trout.

Whole grains are also more complex for your body to break down versus something like processed white bread, which means that you'll end up feeling for longer. For example, you can still enjoy your daily BLT, but instead of using white bread or a white bun, consider replacing that with something like sourdough or 100% whole wheat bread. You can also sneak in extra foods that provide you with energy throughout the day like adding in nuts and seeds. You can enjoy a salad with creamy buttermilk ranch dressing. Just add in a few walnuts as well. You could enjoy having a nightly bowl of ice cream with chocolate and caramel, but consider adding some pecans or chia seeds to help boost your energy levels.

If you're somebody who struggles to maintain a healthy diet or you don't like certain foods, you can also consider adding supplements and other vitamins to your daily routine. These include things like vitamins D and C, omega-3 three fatty acids, or magnesium. These are good for helping to regulate your immune system as well as maintain better mental health.

Try to sneak different foods into other recipes you love, like smoothies or pasta sauces. When you throw things in a blender, it's harder to distinguish different flavors or textures that you might not enjoy. For example, if you are somebody who hates spinach, try blending this up and mixing it into a pesto dish or a breakfast smoothie. By doing this, you can still get the health benefits without having to chew or sometimes even taste those foods that you are a big fan of.

At the end of the day, your mental health matters the most and your brain deserves proper energy, so try and stay focused on providing your body with the energy it needs internally first.

Move Your Body

Much like our nutrition levels, we are told throughout our lives that we have to work out and follow a strict exercise regimen so that our bodies *look* a certain way. In reality, what's important above all else is following physical movement routines to help our mental health more than anything. Humans are primates, which means we have diverse diets. We are omnivores, meaning we hunt and gather things like seeds, nuts, and fruits, in addition to hunting and fishing for animals and fish. This has been a part of our evolution, dating back to the time when we were still primates living in the wild. Because of our diverse diets, we have also developed the need to adapt to a very active lifestyle. Such diverse diets require that we walk through forests and learn how to be strong to fight off predators and prey.

There are some animals in life that don't need to have that much physical movement while still maintaining their health, but humans are not one of them.

We have evolved and adapted over time to need to exercise a certain amount to help burn off our energy. When you live a sedentary lifestyle, it can be very damaging not just to your physical health but to your mental health as well. Sitting for long periods of time can impact the blood flow and level of oxygen that runs through your body. This can make it hard to focus and will eventually reduce cognitive function. Our hormones also require that we exercise, so when you live a sedentary lifestyle, it can increase your stress levels, which will in turn also disrupt your sleep patterns. All of this type of isolation and staying stagnant in the same place can contribute to even more forms of overthinking, increasing your anxiety and decreasing your overall mental health.

Exercise is very impactful to help reduce overthinking for many different reasons. First, and foremost, it can help you reduce stress. The act of actually physically exercising releases endorphins, which help boost your mood and make you feel better overall. This will help you reduce stress. Exercise also maintains energy levels and can be very helpful in making sure that you get better sleep. When you're sitting in the same place all day and you don't get much physical movement, it can be hard to reach that deep restful state of sleep at night. Exercise also improves your physical coordination, which can help with decision-making skills and boost your confidence and motivation levels.

Again, exercise is often associated with looking a certain way, but it's important to overcome the pressures that society has placed on us and instead start thinking about exercise as a means to increase our mental health. Once you do this, it will make it easier to start adding exercise to your daily routine. If you focus on how you *feel* rather than how you *look* after your workout or exercise, it will make it easier to maintain a healthier regimen.

Start by incorporating just five minutes a day of exercise into your daily routine. You don't have to sign up for an expensive gym membership and you don't have to order expensive gym equipment to your home. All you need is a clear space for you to do some things like jumping jacks, squats, or different stretches. You can invest in some smaller equipment as well like a stair stepper, resistance bands, or an exercise ball to help you diversify your workout routine. If you just add five minutes a day for a month, then by the end of the month, exercise becomes a more regular part of your routine. You'll find that once you start exercising, it'll be easier to go for longer than five minutes and you might make it to 15 or 20 minutes.

Wake up in the morning and work out for five minutes. Take a five-minute break during your lunch period to exercise. Exercise for five minutes in between tasks as you're cooking dinner or before you get in the shower. Exercise for five minutes before you go to bed at night!

There are so many small ways you can sneak in a few periods to get in extra movement.

We have this common association with exercise where you have to have the perfect matching spandex outfit and follow the optimal celebrity-endorsed routine with a professional trainer while working out in an expensive gym. But it doesn't have to be like that!

If you build small moments of exercise on top of each other throughout the day it becomes much more natural to incorporate exercise, therefore allowing you to enjoy the benefits of working out. Consider signing up for different classes as well. You might find that you enjoy dance classes or something like karate or boxing. Exercise is also something that you can do in a social setting to help make it more enjoyable while also boosting your motivation to keep pushing through. It might feel uncomfortable at first, especially if you're not somebody who's used to working out, but after a while, you'll find that it's actually a requirement for your day-to-day routine, much like taking a shower or brushing your teeth!

Fix Your Sleep Schedule

The last part of our total health is our sleep schedule. Sleep is something that we've done all of our lives. When we were born, sleep was something that we did most of the day. Sleep is something that is required every day for the rest of our lives, and there is no changing that. While it might not feel like it, there's a good chance that you could be sleep-deprived. Even if you're getting seven hours of sleep a night, it might not be the restful sleep that you need for important restoration processes.

Just like nutrition is important for empowering our brain, sleep is a restorative process that improves your cognitive function overall. If you are tired, it's going to be hard to give things your full attention and retain information. This will end up affecting your memory, so not only will it be harder to recall information when you're tired, but it'll also be harder to store memories when you're tired. This can therefore make you feel more disconnected from the past. When you're focused only on the negative things that you've been through, coupled with poor memory, then it's much easier to fixate on the worst parts of your past alongside your biggest regrets, further perpetuating more overthinking.

A lack of sleep will also exacerbate poor decision-making skills and you'll also likely find yourself struggling with impulsivity. When you're tired, It can be draining and sometimes even painful. You might find yourself struggling with headaches, or a sore jaw from grinding your teeth. You might struggle with body aches and pain, and you might find that your face feels puffy or tired. Your eyes might be red or bloodshot and all of this can make us want to find immediate alleviation.

You might be more impulsive by doing things like skipping class or calling off work. You might find yourself reaching for really sugary energy drinks or coffee drinks to help give you a boost of energy. But as I mentioned earlier, these highly sugary foods are not only addictive, but they don't provide you with long-term energy.

When we are struggling with all these things, it can also make it harder to regulate our emotions. You might find yourself fluctuating between moods of euphoria and then crashing and burning, feeling very lethargic or apathetic. When you are struggling to maintain focus and pay attention, you start to lack interest in the things that you used to enjoy. When you're tired, you might start skipping out on social events or workouts, contributing further to isolation and feeling mentally unwell.

So, what can we do to overcome this? What can we do to start improving our sleep?

Most of us know that we need to get more sleep, we know what it feels like to be tired, and we know the pains of grogginess and struggling to focus. The first thing to do is to understand the power of routine.

Our bodies run on an internal biological clock. This is known as our circadian rhythm. Many animals have a circadian rhythm as well. Consider something like an owl or a spider. When the sun sets, that triggers certain animals to start coming out and hunting for their prey.

Birds, squirrels, and even pets like cats and dogs have a circadian rhythm that helps them regulate their bodily functions throughout the day. They know when it's time to wake up, go to bed, or eat, all based on the sunlight.

We have this circadian rhythm as well, but because of our crazy and chaotic schedules, alongside technology, we are not as in tune with the natural biological system that is built into us. For example, you might be somebody who likes to sleep until noon or later, and you stay up until three in the morning, watching videos on your phone. Whatever schedule you choose to partake in is completely up to you, but when most of your day is spent in the afternoon sun or darkness, that can mess up your body's natural biological system. What's important, above everything else when it comes to sleep, is to maintain consistency in your routine. Ultimately, if you do want to stay up until three in the morning and sleep until noon, that's fine. But keep in mind that consistency is key.

Even though sleeping in on the weekends is enjoyable, it can be beneficial to still get up at the same time to maintain some regulation in your bodily system, especially if you have to wake up at seven in the morning most of the time Monday through Friday.

When you are following a more consistent sleep schedule, it's then easier for your body to go to sleep and reach a deep state of sleep at night, and to wake up earlier in the morning and feel more alert and energized. Your body doesn't always know the difference between 10 minutes or even 15 minutes, so don't fret over going to bed at the exact same time every night. However, if you have to wake up at 7 a.m. most of the time, it's beneficial to try and stick to the same sleep and wake time throughout the week.

It's also important to monitor light usage when you're trying to go to sleep. This is why staying up on your phone and holding it close to your face when you're lying in bed at night can be detrimental to your sleep because you are tricking your brain into thinking that the sun is out.

You can still enjoy some daily social media use, just try to do it in a different room and not in your bed. You should give yourself 20 to 30 minutes to fall asleep before the actual time that you want to go to bed. In addition, exposing yourself to darkness is really important to let your mind and body know that it's time to rest.

Some people do need a nightlight to sleep at night and that's okay, but try to get one that's timed so that once you do fall asleep, that light goes off, and then the rest of the night your body has a better chance of reaching that deep state of sleep. When you wake up in the morning, expose yourself to some sunlight to let your body know that it's time to wake up and get things started for the day.

The four corners of our health are all interconnected, so if you're not eating right, you might not be sleeping right, and if you're not sleeping right, you might not want to work out. When you're not getting a good workout in, you might have poor eating habits, and all of this is going to contribute to your mental health. Try and focus on troubleshooting the things that you are not doing at the moment to help you get a better idea of how to maintain your overall health to reduce mental chatter. It's not always outside circumstances that are contributing to mental chatter, but rather, the system inside of our body and how we're maintaining that which can make it challenging to silence our loudest thoughts.

Chapter Review

At the end of the day, we are biological machines with specific needs. We require certain inputs and therefore create certain outputs. I'm not just talking about your digestive system either! What we eat can impact how we think, and that will impact how we act. How we act can therefore impact what we eat, thus creating a cycle that determines our physical and mental wellbeing.

Learn how to manage your total health with the methods below:

1. **Empower your mind and body with brain-boosting foods for total nutrition.** The fuel you give your body will help you ensure you stay focused and energized throughout the day. Remember that certain foods do not have to be demonized. Total nutrition is all about balance.

2. **Incorporate exercise as a regular part of daily life.** We are genetically wired to need and use a certain amount of physical exercise. We can't change our operating system, but we can utilize exercise in any way that works for our total health.

3. **Sync up with a healthy sleep schedule.** How much rest we give to our bodies will determine a lot when it comes to how our brain functions. Sometimes you might simply feel groggy with brain fog because you are tired! When you determine what is causing a lack of healthy sleep, it then becomes easier to create a schedule that works for you.

When trying to quiet the thoughts that clutter your mind, your first wish might be for a new brain! However, you can help your brain become the best version possible by troubleshooting different habits you have with your body. Pay attention to the four corners of health to ensure the framework for mental clarity is taken care of. Utilizing mindfulness isn't just a temporary thing. Set up your future for success by taking on new habits and being proactive with your health.

The process of becoming more mindful isn't going to happen overnight. It happens through small, specialized instances that create a solid foundation for continuous growth. Life will keep flowing, so rather than getting stuck on a rock in this river of life, we can use mindfulness to help us build a boat that will carry us downstream.

Chapter 7:

Future Strategies for Long-Lasting Growth

Mindfulness is something to continue doing even after we start to feel like we have more control over our thoughts. Overthinking can return, even when it seems like it's under control. It only takes one small thought to spiral into a territory of mental chatter. We have an estimate of at least 6,000 thoughts per day (Raypole, 2022). That means we have thousands of opportunities to spiral into a dark territory of fear, worry, and panic.

Going forward, it's helpful to have a strategy in place so you know exactly what to do if the cyclone of endless thoughts begins. This way, you can ensure an anxious thought doesn't ruin your day.

It's natural to experience stress. It's a survival tactic! It helps ensure we stay focused on a positive future while raising awareness of our surroundings. What's most important is knowing how to utilize this stress to overcome obstacles rather than letting it become an additional pain point. There are plenty of things to be stressed about in life, but there are just as many beautiful things to admire. Life is about finding the balance to ensure our mental strength is louder than the chatter.

Get Creative

We recently discussed the importance of being creative in group settings, but beyond that, it's also helpful to explore your creative side individually. In addition, recall the discussion of how you have the right and left sides of your brain, and how the right side is focused on creativity. We have to use logic in many things we do. We have to use logic to get most of our work tasks done or think analytically in school studies. We also have to think logically when doing things like domestic duties or problem-solving within our relationships.

Unless you are somebody who's artistic on their own, you might not explore your creative side as often as you should or at least as often as you do your logical side. This can lead to an imbalance in your mentality, disrupting the flow of your thoughts.

Flex the other side of your brain by getting creative and learning how to explore the innovative side of life. Creativity is a way that we can challenge our brains. We have to come up with fresh ideas and think of new innovations. This can help build our problem-solving skills because we are training our brains to come up with new resolutions. Creativity is also a way that we can become adaptive. For example, if you are cleaning out your home, you might find a bunch of things that you thought were useless; but through the use of creativity, you can use them to build something new, that therefore becomes useful. Most importantly, art and creativity are great outlets for exploring our emotional side. Many of the greatest artists of all time used artwork as a way to express what they were feeling without having to put it into words.

Art is something that's universal and not dependent on one specific regimen, set of rules, or a general basis of how we should be creative. This freedom to express ourselves and explore the deeper parts of our brain can help reduce stress and enable us to make more sense of ourselves and the world around us. Creativity also helps you see things from new perspectives, which can make it easier to be more open-minded. It allows you to understand that there might be a deeper meaning hidden behind what you see on the surface.

It allows us to break through preconceived notions and discover new parts of ourselves. To help you become more creative, first and foremost, start exploring the creative side of yourself that you enjoy the most. Are you somebody who's always connected to painting? Do you prefer to play instruments and explore your musical side? Are you more of an observant person and do you like to read or watch movies? While you aren't necessarily creating anything, you're still exploring your creative side by immersing yourself in these types of artwork.

Once you find something that you enjoy, then flourish this and practice it consistently. Afterward, it's time to challenge yourself. Try and do something creative that you might not have thought you liked. For example, if you're somebody who doesn't enjoy messes, try something like finger painting or sculpting with clay. It might be really uncomfortable at first, but you could find through time that this is a great way to help you explore your creativity and express yourself.

Remember that creativity is also something we can do with our bodies, whether that's through acting or dancing. Try and put yourself out there and experiment with these different forms of creativity. Do you have a talent you can showcase at a local open mic night? Next time you're home alone, turn up the volume on the radio and dance to whatever song pops up.

Lastly, when it comes to being creative, it's important that we also learn how to share the creations that we make. You don't have to open up and share every single thing that you create. However, it can be really helpful to boost your motivation and improve confidence to be able to share something that you're proud of. Challenge yourself to share something on social media that you make. This can help you stay focused and dedicated to the artwork while also offering yourself up to potential criticism or praise.

The creative process is something we should do for ourselves. However, putting ourselves out there is a great way to overcome perfectionist tendencies and reduce our insecurity. Once you put yourself out there, you'll realize that a lot of people enjoy what you have to share and they're a lot more kind and welcoming than you might have initially thought. When you allow yourself to embrace a creative mindset, you allow yourself to explore a new avenue in life. This can be very beneficial to help you rework the mental chatter that has been keeping you stagnant in the same place.

Do What You Hate

Going forward, one thing that you can do to help you focus on reducing mental chatter is to know the difference between a growth mindset and a fixed mindset. Let's start first by discussing what a fixed mindset is. A fixed mindset is one that kind of perpetuates the same mental patterns over and over again, without making any attempt to escape them. You might be struggling with cognitive distortions and finding yourself cycling through the same patterns, but wanting to break free is a good sign that you can foster a growth mindset.

Fixed mindsets reduce our ability to transform and explore new areas of our brain. They're very limiting to our potential and keep us stuck in the same place. Fixed mindsets are focused on the negative aspect, assuming the worst and failing to believe in our real abilities.

Fixed mindsets are very static, and believe a sort of "it is what it is" mentality in that they might believe that we're given a certain brain and that's just what we have to work with. Fixed mindsets might not believe that it's possible to change for the better and won't attempt to do so.

Fixed mindsets are very afraid of growth and often perpetuate the fear of failure. They will believe that it's easier to just keep doing what you're doing if it's working, rather than trying to improve, even if it means something better could result from those attempts at change.

Fixed mindsets are very afraid of trying new things. For example, somebody with a fixed mindset might not want to try and learn how to play a new game, or they might order the same thing at every restaurant they go to because they don't care to try new things.

It's not that they try things and don't like them. It's just that they fail to try things at all from the start. It's okay if you have certain preferences, but it's also important to explore new things to help our minds continue to grow. Those who struggle with a fixed mindset can become very easily defeated and struggle with resilience. For example, somebody with a fixed mindset who gets bad news might give up. They might not want to bother trying to change or improve things for the better.

Somebody with a growth mindset is the complete opposite. They'll see the setbacks or adversity as a chance to power through and learn something new. They're not afraid of failure, and they understand that even if they do fail, that's an opportunity for them to learn something. Those with growth mindsets explore new things, and even if they find that they don't like these new things, they keep trying. Somebody with a growth mindset might order something new at a restaurant every time they go. Even if they don't like that dish, they'll still keep trying new things because they want to explore the world and take on as many opportunities as possible.

How can we foster a growth mindset? Fixed mindsets can be comfortable, though they don't necessarily help us improve or be the best versions of ourselves. They provide safety in that we find something that works and we stick to it, even if it's not the best method possible. To foster a growth mindset, we have to be willing to be uncomfortable. We have to explore the discomfort of the world and be okay with that in the end, and know that no matter what happens, everything is going to work out.

Those with growth minds know they have to be patient and understand that the first attempt they try something new might not be the best. They can keep getting back up and trying again until they find something that works. Somebody with a growth mindset isn't afraid of feedback. They're willing to take criticism because they want to be the best version of themselves. They want to keep trying and finding something that works for them.

As you keep going forward, you want to focus on how you can grow your mindset to help stifle the chatter that you're stuck with now. Think of your mind like a garden. Right now, you are stuck within a garden box and the weeds (mental chatter) are taking over. Rather than just plucking the weeds, let yourself outgrow the garden box. Spread past the barriers and become so strong that you overtake the weeds, letting your blossoms flourish.

There are a few things you can try to do to help you let this growth mindset expand. First and foremost, do something that you thought you disliked. Do something that you hate. Try food that you think is gross. Listen to a song by an artist you thought you disliked or do something else that, in the past, you may be looked down upon. Go back and rediscover this with a new lens.

You might find that you still dislike this musical artist or you think that food is still gross, but at least you challenged yourself to step outside of your comfort zone. When we are willing to make ourselves uncomfortable, that is when it becomes easier to do things like confront overthinking and the mental roadblocks that keep us in the same place.

Another thing you can do is learn something new. Whether it's a small skill, a new card game, or something big like a new language, learning something new is a great way to help you grow your knowledge. We often leave learning up to those in authority positions, whether that's our teacher or our boss, but learning is something we should be doing on our own and it can come from within us to help us create a new world for ourselves and our mindset.

Challenge yourself to step outside of your comfort zone and do something that you might think you would fail at. If you've never rollerbladed in your life, try rollerblading. If you've never stepped on a skateboard, try stepping on a skateboard! Doing these things is a way for us to boost our confidence and know that even if we fall on our butts, we'll be able to get back up and keep going.

This will help you push through mental chatter. When you hear that voice inside your head saying that you're not good enough or that you're going to fail, you can use these experiences as a reminder that you just need to dust yourself off and keep trying.

Get Mindful Through Grounding

The last method of overcoming mental chatter that I want to provide you with is the use of grounding. Grounding is the act of placing yourself physically within the present moment. One simple way to do this right now is to place both of your feet flat on the ground. You are literally grounding yourself by putting the bottom of your foot against the surface of the area that is supporting you right now. This is a reminder to your physical body that you are here in the moment. You're physically safe and you're steady.

If you were in the water, and the waves were crashing over you, you might want to find your footing to make sure that you stay level-headed. When our thoughts are all over the place, dizzying us in the process, then grounding is a reminder that you are going to be okay.

Grounding is a way for you to physically bring yourself into the moment, so therefore, your mentality will eventually follow. When you can tell your body *I am right here and I am okay right now*, then your thoughts will eventually fade away from whatever past anxieties they're circling through, or whatever future fears it's focused on. There are many different types of grounding activities that you can do to help you increase mindfulness in the present moment.

The first one I want to talk about is the use of a grounding object. A grounding object is something physical that serves as a reminder that you are in the present moment. The next time that you are feeling really happy, positive, and mindful, find a small object that you can utilize as your grounding object. Hold on to this and enjoy all of the good feelings that come along with being mindful. Channel all of your energy and thoughts into the small object. Then place it with you in an important area, whether that's your coat pocket or your purse. The next time that you're feeling anxious, or your mind is spiraling through mental chatter, you can reach for this grounding object and hold on to it in your hand. Squeeze it hard and let all those thoughts and good feelings flood back to you to serve as a reminder that you are okay and everything is going to eventually fade.

This grounding object is a physical point for you to connect to and to help fulfill your need for peace and clarity. Another great grounding object you can use is a stone. Step outside and find a stone in your garden or go on a nature walk and find a unique-looking rock. You can then also paint this using basic craft paint or even nail polish is also a great option. Some brands of nail polish are meant to provide a glossy look without chipping, so it could be useful for long-term use. Paint the stone with pretty colors or even write a mantra on it to help remind you to stay grounded in the moment. Any other pocket-sized trinket is also a great grounding object, like keychains, chapstick, or coins. If something has a scent or a specific texture, that can also be very powerful and help you stay grounded.

Another type of grounding exercise and one that can help you connect to nature is the use of forest bathing. Forest bathing is a practice from Japanese culture that involves spending time in nature and completely immersing yourself in this green environment. What this requires is that you immerse yourself in a completely natural space, whether it's a forest or a nature preserve. It should be somewhere that has trees and grass and many natural sounds. You'll then want to make sure that you put all electronic devices away including any music.

Many people like to listen to music or podcasts when they're going on walks, but for forest bathing, make sure that you put all these additional sounds away. In addition, you'll want to make sure that you practice some deep breathing exercises while here. Try the alternate nostril method or deep belly breathing to help you connect to nature. It's also really helpful to focus on walking incredibly slowly and taking each step as leisurely as possible. The slower you walk, the more you will be able to soak up the natural environment around you.

The last grounding method I want to talk about is the use of ice baths. Previously, I mentioned holding an ice cube and watching it melt away. The coldness of the ice cube can be very shocking to our nervous system, which should make it easier to snap out of a mentally foggy mindset and instead point to this present moment. One simple way to do this is to simply take a cold shower. Next time you find yourself endlessly ruminating or you can't stop thinking about something that's making you anxious, step into a cold shower. You don't necessarily have to wash yourself off, especially if you've already showered, so you don't have to worry about shampooing your hair or using soap. You can just simply step into the icy cold shower and picture washing away all of your thoughts as the water shocks your system.

Another method is to use an ice bowl to dunk your face into. Fill a bowl with ice and water. Then, in five-second to 10-second intervals, immerse your face into that bowl. Make sure you hold your breath and don't take a deep breath in. Once you dunk your head in, it can be easy to want to take a breath because your system becomes shocked, but you'll want to make sure you keep your eyes and mouth closed as you do this. Lastly, you can take an entire ice bath. Fill your tub with ice and cold water and then immerse your body for anywhere between five to 30 seconds. You don't want to spend too long in there to not stress your body out, but immersing your entire body in this tub is a great way for you to power through pain and discomfort and learn how to connect back to your body.

Grounding is a very powerful technique that will help you reduce mental chatter while allowing you to empower yourself in the present moment.

Chapter Review

Mindfulness isn't just a tool to use going forward. It is a feature you can build into your thought process! As long as you keep up with these mindful practices, you will notice the fogginess of mental chatter starts to clear. There will be ups and downs in your thought process. That's normal and to be expected! Our health and hormones fluctuate, so of course our thoughts will as well. What's important is reminding yourself that no matter the intensity of the storm, it will pass and you will come out on the other side.

The three final ways to reduce mental chatter covered in this book are:

1. **Explore your creative side. We all have some form of creativity, even if it doesn't seem that way.** Creativity isn't

always about making something artistic like a painting or sculpture. Try new meals, garden, and create a dance routine!

2. **Do things you thought you hated. While it might seem as though you disliked something, you might discover you actually like this!** Alternatively, you can foster self-reflection by confronting the things you believed you disliked.

3. **Physically ground yourself.** Find a metaphorical magnet you can use to pull you into the present. By doing this, you enable yourself to snap into a more focused and mental presence.

While I've provided 21 methods to become more mindful throughout the readings, these are not the only ways you can increase your mindfulness! Keep learning, exploring, and growing. There's a big world out there, and the possibilities for positive change are endless.

Conclusion

Above all, we cannot afford not to live in the present. —Henry David Thoreau

Life is too short and beautiful for us to be stuck in the negative world our mind perpetuates through excessive mental chatter. Shed the shackles of your worst thoughts and let the ideas of happiness start to flow!

Mindfulness is not something that can be gained overnight. It can be improved fairly quickly, but it requires consistent practice. There is no one, singular way to be mindful. The best thing to do moving forward is to maintain a high level of mindfulness through several methods at once.

Below, I've collected the 21 methods of improving mindfulness to reduce overthinking I've covered in the book. This checklist provides a basis for you to build more mindfulness throughout daily life:

1. Understand mindfulness at its core to help you make the most of this practice.

2. Utilize breathwork and breathing exercises to calm your stress response.

3. Practice meditating for more mental control, peace, and clarity.

4. Identify common thought patterns you've been struggling with and any mental cycles that have been keeping you trapped.

5. Start journaling to help keep track of your thoughts and make more sense of them.

6. Identify negative affirmations and replace them with neutral and positive ones to rework the voice in your head.

7. Know the difference between the left and right sides of your brain and practice different methods of connecting both.

8. Utilize reframing as a way to see things from a new perspective.

9. Tap into all five of your senses to create more mindful sensory immersive experiences.

10. Practice mindful eating to make the most out of each meal and snack.

11. Change up your physical space by decluttering or redecorating to make it easier to create a new mindset.

12. Organize tasks and chunk them together while also utilizing timers to make it easier to avoid procrastination and stay on track.

13. Recognize your body language and the language of others to foster deeper and more meaningful communication.

14. Use weekly mindfulness activities, like screen-free days, to help your household become more mindful together.

15. Get creative in a group setting to learn new things and explore a different side of each other.

16. Check in with the fuel you're providing to your body and consider if this is contributing to mental chatter.

17. Add in more moments of physical movement to decrease stress and alleviate some of the things that drive overthinking.

18. Stay on a stricter sleep schedule and reduce screen time before bed to help improve your total health.

19. Spend more time with your creative side to explore new ways of thinking while also helping yourself express more emotions.

20. Foster a growth mindset and consider trying something you hate to challenge comfortability.

21. Practice more grounding techniques to help you remind your mind and body that you are okay in this present moment.

It's easy to lose motivation, especially if a method doesn't seem to work, but remember to push through your thoughts because, eventually, it will all click.

Once you start to become more mindful, it's hard to go back to your old way of thinking. It might seem like a distant dream, but one day, you will lead with mindfulness. You will start to enjoy the beauty of the world while strengthening your appreciation of life. Mindfulness is like a superpower, helping you to combat your most negative thoughts, improve relationships, and increase productivity all by using your own mind.

Start this process now and uncover the secrets of living in the present. You only have one life to live and one mind to enjoy this life with, so do what you can to nurture it for long-lasting joy.

References

Ankrom, S. (2023, April 1). *Anxiety and GI issues: What's the connection?* Verywell Mind. https://www.verywellmind.com/gastrointestinal-gi-symptoms-and-anxiety-disorders-2584240

Aurelius, M. (2006). *Meditations.* Dover Publications.

Chapman, C. & Teichroeb, J. (2012). *What influences the size of groups in which primates choose to live?* The Nature Education. https://www.nature.com/scitable/knowledge/library/what-influences-the-size-of-groups-in-58068275/

Dark, T., Flynn, H., Harman, J., Kinsell, H., & Rust, G. (2016, October 17). *Epidemiology of emergency department visits for anxiety in the United States: 2009-2011.* National Library of Medicine. https://pubmed.ncbi.nlm.nih.gov/27745531/

Harlow, O. (n.d.). *Fun facts about the brain that will blow your mind.* Analog. https://legacybox.com/blogs/analog/25-brain-facts-blow-mind

Novotney, A. (2019). *The risks of social isolation.* American Psychological Association. https://www.apa.org/monitor/2019/05/ce-corner-isolation

Raypole, C. (2022, February 28). *How many thoughts do you have each day? And other things to think about.* Healthline. https://www.healthline.com/health/how-many-thoughts-per-day

Sander, L. (2019, January 25). *What does clutter do to your brain and body?* RACGP. https://www1.racgp.org.au/newsgp/clinical/what-does-clutter-do-to-your-brain-and-body

Thoreau, H. D. (1862). *Walking.* Gutenberg. https://www.gutenberg.org/cache/epub/1022/pg1022-images.html

Printed in Great Britain
by Amazon

40304214R00059